"In this book pioneer responsible investor ~~and asset manager, Terry Mollner,~~ leads us toward the likely future of capitalism. We agree that cooperation is the framework for all human activities and especially in the evolution of markets and corporations. Based on his deep experience, Mollner describes how corporations, while fully doing both, will progress toward giving priority to the common good and second priority to competition."

Dr. Hazel Henderson —
author of *Mapping the Global Transition to the Solar Age*,
President of Ethical Markets Media (USA & Brazil), a Certified B Corporation

"Open the morning paper, turn on Netflix, or browse Amazon – you don't have to look very far to find corporation as villain, for their real and perceived damage done to all of us. Against this angry backdrop, Common Good Capitalism Is Inevitable *offers an olive branch, presenting companies a clear and pragmatic path forward to transform from villain to hero.*
Terry Mollner's startlingly clear vision gives me faith that perhaps there is hope for us yet."

Upendra Shardanand —
Co-founder of Firefly Network, The Accelerator Group, and Daylife

"Terry is an inspirational figure and a true social entrepreneur. This book takes you on a ride through our personal layers of maturity and how we sometimes fail to realize that as members of any society, however structured, our priority is the common good. Terry reveals how businesses in a product sector can unite—like the teams in a baseball league—to reach common good agreements, monitor each other's behavior by providing annual common good audits, and continue to secondly compete. He is right. If we want to build on free markets and sustain public support, this is the way businesses will eventually voluntarily give priority to the common good. As "duopoly monopolies," as he calls them, continue to spread and become known by the public, for businesses to continue to survive and thrive this pattern of thinking and sports league model will be crucial to be in harmony with both the ecosystem and this natural human society priority"

Gurmat Raunaq Sahni —
Co-founder of Grand Slam Baseball, India

Common Good Capitalism is Inevitable

It is the only economic model
that both builds on free markets and
represents our next layer of maturity in
the skill of self-consciousness.

TERRY MOLLNER

The Love Skill Publishing

Cover design and text and layout: Greg Caulton

Printed by CreateSpace.com

Common Good Capitalism is Inevitable / Terry Mollner

ISBN-13: 9781530821600
ISBN-10: 1530821606

Printed in the United States of America

Any views expressed in this book, *Common Good Capitalism is Inevitable,* are my own and do not necessarily reflect those of the Calvert Funds, Calvert Investment Management, Inc. or my fellow Trustees/Directors on the Calvert Funds Boards or Calvert Foundation; nor those of StakeHolders Capital, Inc.

$19.95 US

CONTENTS

Contents

For our Earth society.

Change Is Difficult and Effortful
Maturation Is Easy and Effortless

Change is difficult and effortful.
To stop eating too much, consistent effort is necessary.
To stop buying more than we need, consistent effort is necessary.

Maturation is easy and effortless.
From the moment we begin to walk, we stop crawling.
From the moment we learn to ride a bicycle, we stop falling off of it.
From the moment we learn to use chopsticks with one hand, we stop
    using them with two hands.

From the moment we learn we have the ability and right of individual
    freedom of choice, we do not easily give our power to another.
From the moment we learn that our most important free choice is
    our fundamental belief, because whether or not we are aware
    of it we are always operating on one, we choose one.
From the moment we learn the universe is an indivisible whole,
    we choose this as our fundamental belief: moral behavior.
From the moment we learn even choosing it is giving our power to a
    second thing that does not actually exist, a belief, we give priority
    to the experience of it: enlightenment.
From the moment we learn there is not a higher layer of maturity
    in the skill of self-consciousness than this, we give priority to
    participation in the maturation of us all: eldering.

And, from the moment we learn that food is primarily for sustenance
    and secondly for pleasure we stop eating too much.
And, from the moment we learn shopping is primarily for adequacy
    and secondly for pleasure we donate more for the common good.

Change is difficult and effortful.
Maturation is easy and effortless.

Common Good Capitalism

MANIFESTO

Any time two people come together they have two choices: to compete or cooperate. If they choose to compete, they are in a constant state of conflict. Not fun. If they choose to cooperate they have used their human skill of self-consciousness to make an *agreement*. The agreement is that they will give priority to the common good of the two of them as if they are two parts of a whole. This can be what we label "friendship," "romantic love," or "partnership." This can be great fun.

When many people choose to do this, we call it "a society."

It does not make any difference how the society is structured: as a group of friends, village, dictatorship, communist state, or democracy. Self-interest is still expected and encouraged…as a second priority. However, only as a second priority. In any society all have agreed to give highest priority to the common good. Anyone who does not do so has left the society and is now in competition with it.

As people in business become aware of this they will choose common good capitalism: cooperative competition. They will use the sports league model. The competitors in a product market will meet, agree on some "common good rules of play," provide annual common good as well as financial audits by creditable third parties so all can see that all competitors are keeping their agreements, and secondly compete as ferociously as before.

Thus, while honoring individual freedom and free markets, the freely chosen priority in the private sector is the common good. It is what is best for all stakeholders including the shareholders, employees, community, and environment.

This is also the mutual expression of our maturation into the next layer of maturity in the skill of self-consciousness: the recognition of the oneness of nature. Therefore, it is inevitable.

Introduction

THERE IS A REASON I COMFORTABLY DECLARE IN THE TITLE OF this book that "common good capitalism is inevitable": it is the economic expression of the next layer of maturity in the skill of self-consciousness into which many of us are ready and able to mature.

As we all know well, when we find a better way to do anything we can't easily keep ourselves from turning it into a skill and then a habit that replaces our old habit. For instance, when we find a more time-saving and enjoyable route to drive to work we immediately begin to use it. It is the same with our economy. When we find a more mature way to operate it, we will not be able to stop ourselves from doing it. I believe common good capitalism is the economic expression of the next layer of maturity in the skill of self-consciousness into which we, as a human species, will eventually mature. Therefore, I think it is inevitable.

In this *Introduction*, I will begin by presenting an editorial by me that summarizes how our corporate community has found a legal way to effect monopoly behavior, what is referred to as "duopoly monopolies." Three very visible examples are CVS-Walgreens, Lowe's-Home Depot, and MasterCard-Visa. A monopoly is illegal but a duopoly, where two companies control a large percentage of a product market, is legal. Then, *without ever talking to each other*, they can orchestrate monopoly behavior by matching each other's fundamental price increases. Thus, it is not done through direct collusion that is illegal. They will then continue to compete as their second priority. And since this is technically legal, all companies are scrambling to become number one or two in their product markets or get out of them. *They know they do not have a choice.* If they don't do it, two other companies will accomplish it.

When the public becomes aware of this, we will feel trapped. It will eventually be discovered that the common good capitalism solution presented herein is the *only* one that builds on individual freedom and free markets which we will not want to end. This is a second reason I am confident its emergence is eventually inevitable.

In the second half of this *Introduction* I will briefly describe the maturation in the skill of self-consciousness that will have it be inevitable. The rest of this book will provide further explanation of what is presented in this *Introduction*. It will also describe the voluntary route solely in the private sector that will be used to transition into common good capitalism.

On July 11 and 12, 2016, the following Guest Editorial by me, in two sections, was published in the *Daily Hampshire Gazette* in Northampton, MA with the title "What kind of movement, Bernie?" It was a call for Senator Bernie Sanders to launch both a *common good movement* as well as a *political movement.* He subsequently lost his campaign to be the Democratic Party nominee for President of the USA to Hillary Clinton. However he has continued his "revolution" under the title "Our Revolution" (www.ourrevolution.com). It is a political movement. It is primarily a call for certain policies to receive legislative support and for the election of candidates who will move them forward.

However, successful political movements are usually an extension of a common good movement, a moral movement.

The latter is a movement to mature something in the way we all think, for instance that we switch to thinking of people of color and women as worthy of equal rights with, respectfully, whites and men: Civil Rights and Women's Movements. Common good movements argue for a voluntary change of what has been an acceptable social behavior that we have now matured to know is immoral. It is not freely choosing to give priority to the common good. In above examples, it is affirming that all human beings deserve equal rights. Regardless of how a society is structured, always giving priority to the common good is our most fundamental agreement with each other. Eventually, with widespread support these maturations in the thinking of most of us are also given expression in legislation. For instance, the Civil Rights Act of 1964.

As you will see, this book is a call for the emergence of a common good movement called the "Common Good Capitalism Movement," or for short, the "Common Good Movement." It argues that giving priority in business activities to the financial interests of a few is immoral—not fair. It is not giving priority to the common good. It is welcomed and encouraged as a second priority. *Within the keeping of this fundamental agreement,* this allows for and encourages individual freedom of expression and creativity.

However, to fulfill this most fundamental agreement with each other as members of a society, the freely chosen priority of individuals and groups needs to always be the common good.

This book also describes the route that will be used, solely within the private sector and building on individual freedom, freely chosen agreements, and free markets, to mature capitalism into common good capitalism where everyone experiences themselves as winning.

Finally, like the Civil Rights and Women's Movements, the purpose of the Common Good Movement is to speed up the inevitable: our maturation into ending by the free choice of us all an acceptable social tradition that is not giving priority to the common good and replacing it with one that does give priority to the common good.

The following is an updated and improved version of the above Guest Editorial:

WHAT KIND OF MOVEMENT, BERNIE?

Even though Senator Bernie Sanders has lost the Democratic Party nomination for President, he has made a commitment to continuing his "revolution." This raises the question: "Will the vehicle for it be a common good movement, political movement, or both?"

Like Mahatma Gandhi, Martin Luther King Jr., and Nelson Mandela, to be successful it needs to be both. They each need the other. Let me describe them and, in particular, why a political movement needs to be based on a common good movement.

A political movement is when people come together *to move some policies into legislation.* It includes electing candidates to help do it.

A common good movement is when people come together to mature something in the way we all think. We have matured to where we can see that an acceptable social behavior is immoral—not fair. It is not in alignment with our commitment to give priority to the common good. Therefore, we can't choose to do it or not do it.

As a society, we must all freely choose to stop doing it as an expression of our commitment to give priority to the common good.

The Civil Rights Movement is a common good movement. We have matured to know it is immoral—not fair—to deny blacks and people of color equal rights with white people.

The Women's Movement is a common good movement. We have matured to know it is immoral—not fair—to deny women equal rights with men.

The Environment Movement is a common good movement. We have matured to know it is immoral—not fair—to risk ending human life on Earth for our children's children.

The goal of these common good movements is to mature something in the way we *all* think: *to freely choosing to keep our agreement to give priority to the common good.*

They all also resulted in legislation that supported them. However, without the foundation of a common good movement it would not have been possible to eventually succeed in having the political movements be successful. And without the political movements the common good movements would only have been aspirational movements rather than grounded in new agreements that reflected maturations in thinking.

The foundation of a common good movement is easy to understand. Allow me to describe it.

Any time two people come together they have two choices: to compete or co-operate. If they choose to compete, they are in a constant state of conflict. Not fun. If they choose to cooperate they have used their human skill of self-consciousness to make an *agreement*. The agreement is that they will give priority to the common good of the two of them as if they are two parts of a whole. This can be what we label "friendship," "romantic love," or "partnership." This can be great fun.

When many people choose to do this, we call it "a society."

It does not make any difference how the society is structured: as a group of friends, village, dictatorship, communist state, or democracy. Also, self-interest is still fine and dandy…and expected and encouraged…*as a second priority.* However, only as a second priority. As a member of a society at all times the highest priority is the common good.

This is the fundamental agreement of all the members of a society.

For fun and creativity, competition can be second in priority. This is how sports leagues operate, both local ones like a child's soccer league and large ones like the National Basketball Association (NBA). The competing teams meet, agree on the "rules of the game," and hire referees who make sure *the agreements are always given priority during the games.* Giving priority to self-interest, particularly by finding a clever way to get around them, is breaking this most fundamental agreement to give priority to the agreed upon "common good rules of play."

It is the same in a society. If a person's highest priority *is anything other than the common good,* that person has left the society and is then in competition with it. We have a word for this. We call it a "crime."

For instance, killing and stealing are not giving priority to the common good. They are giving priority to self-interest. Therefore, we call them "crimes."

In a society, there are two kinds of crimes: illegal and legal crimes. *Illegal crimes* are those, like killing and stealing, that have been declared in the laws of the society as not acceptable; it has been agreed that they do not give priority to the common good. *Legal crimes* are crimes that have not yet been made illegal in laws.

The purpose of a common good movement is to expose a currently legal crime so citizens both choose to not do it anymore and laws can be passed that make it illegal.

We have matured to where we can now see that that particular acceptable behavior is not giving priority to the common good and, therefore, we have an obligation as members of the society to do our best to persuade all other members to freely choose to not do it anymore. This is the main activity of a Common Good Movement.

Regarding the equal rights of all human beings, the purpose of the Civil Rights Movement is to end the acceptable behavior, the legal crime, of treating people of color different than white people. The purpose of the Women's Movement is to end the acceptable behavior, the legal crime, or treating women different than men. The purpose of the Environment Movement is to end the acceptable behavior, the legal crime, of not accepting responsibility for sustaining the possibility of human life for our children's children.

Each is assisting in the maturation of the thinking of us all to where we freely choosing to give priority to the common good where we have not been doing it. Then, eventually and supported by nearly all, laws are passed that make not giving priority to the common good in that particular area illegal.

Mahatma Gandhi taught us that the only time it is not only good but also our responsibility to not cooperate with an existing agreement within a society is when it is immoral—not fair, not giving priority to the common good. If we are unsuccessful using persuasion, as with the Civil Rights, Women's, and Environment Movements, we have an obligation *to openly and directly not cooperate with immoral behavior* as part of our responsibility to always give priority to the common good in our society. Gandhi and his movement did not cooperate with England's colonialization of India. Martin Luther King Jr. and the Civil Rights Movement stopped cooperating with blacks having to sit in the back of the bus or not being allowed to sit at "whites only" lunch counters.

Gandhi also knew that, no matter how long the struggle, the society would eventually embrace the maturation being sought. Maturation is a constant. When it is clearly understood that the change is to a more mature way of being as individuals and a society, eventually all freely choose to make the change for an obvious reason: *more mature behavior is always more enjoyable than less mature behavior.*

It is more enjoyable to walk than to crawl, to ride a bicycle to more quickly than walking get from one place to another, or to use chopsticks with one hand rather than with two hands. It is also more enjoyable to relate with people of color and women as having equal rights with us all because we are all equally human beings and it is honoring that fact and being able to enjoy it. It also ends being in conflict with some people because of an immature and immoral social tradition that naturally stimulates conflict because it is not giving priority to the common good.

Today, in America and much of the world there is *another important acceptable behavior in our societies that is immoral—not fair, a legal crime.* Many of us have matured to see that it is, indeed, immoral—not giving priority to the common good of our societies. Therefore, we have an obligation to do our best to persuade all in these societies that we must stop doing it. And if unsuccessful using persuasion, we must not cooperate with its existence until all see the responsibility to embrace the more mature choice. Let me describe it for you.

Wall Street and corporate America believe they have been granted the equivalent of an exemption to this highest priority of us all. They believe their highest priority can be the financial interests of a few, usually labeled the "owners" or "shareholders." Since this will provide some benefits and costs to society, and *because they value the personal and social benefits more than the costs,* they do not think they need to be sure they are *directly at all times giving priority to the common good.* They are mistaken, wrong.

To give priority at any time to anything other than the common good is immoral, not fair. It is a crime. Within a society, it is a breaking of our most fundamental agreement with each other.

In doing so they have left our society and are now in competition with it. Although this is currently sanctioned as "legal," as acceptable, it is actually "a legal crime." It is not giving priority to the common good.

Therefore, a common good movement is needed to assist us all to mature to freely choose to stop doing it.

To be fair, our awakening to this fact is in part the result of the emergence of the Information Age. It has allowed something new to occur few of us anticipated.

Up until now companies existed in silos with little knowledge of what was occurring in their competitors' companies. So our agreement was that each company was assumed to be giving priority to the common good and second priority to profits *in a level playing field marketplace.* Of course, to sustain a level playing field this included not being in collusion with some competitors for mutual self-interest. There were also laws that made such direct collusion illegal. It was also based on the assumption by many that we are each separate from one another and, therefore, by nature give priority to our self-interest.

This ignores the fact that we have also used our human skill of self-consciousness to agree to be members of a society, that is, to agree to always give priority to the common good.

Thus, beginning in the 1970s, especially as a result of the influence of the economist Milton Freidman and, more importantly, some people's interpretation of his teachings, executives came to belief their highest priority was the financial interests of a few, their company's owners or shareholders.

It was the government that was responsible for making sure that all gave priority to the common good, not them.

This belief, in combination with the emergence of the Information Age, has resulted in something not anticipated that is a legal crime: *duopoly monopolies.*

A duopoly monopoly is where two companies control such a large percentage of a product market that, without ever talking to each other, they can jointly and legally execute monopoly behavior. Therefore, technically, it is not illegal because it is not "direct collusion."

They primarily and easily do it by giving priority to matching each other's fundamental price increases. Now their priority is their mutual self-interest. As groups within our societies this is a clear breach of their commitment to give priority to the common good.

This is another legal crime. Therefore, it is now the responsibility of those of us who understand how this is occurring to become part of a common good movement to end it.

Just as the Civil Rights, Women's, and Environment Movements demanded an end to social traditions that we had matured to know are legal crimes, this common good movement will demand an end to the legal crime of giving priority to profit for a few.

By the way, when it comes to the maturation of our societies we most easily assume politicians are the most powerful, corporations the second most powerful, consumers the third most powerful, and movements the least powerful. *It is the exact opposite.* As indicated above, the purpose of a common good movement is to mature something in the way we all think. That eventually matures consumer behavior. That eventually matures corporate behavior. And the politicians are the last to act, that is, to pass legislation in support of it. This usually does not happen until most of the people in the country support the change.

Thus, a common good movement is the most powerful force for the maturation of the freely chosen behavior of individuals and groups in societies. And this eventually results in legislation (agreements) that make it illegal to not give priority to the common good in that particular area.

The current problem is that since duopoly monopolies are legal, it is clear to all in the corporate community that if one's company does not become number one or two in its product market two other companies will achieve it, achieve a duopoly monopoly. Therefore, it has to be pursued or it is better to get out of that product market and only be in those where one's company can achieve a duopoly or triopoly monopoly.

As societies, our first mistake was to allow ourselves to believe we could separate the responsibility we all have to keep our most fundamental agreement to give priority to the common good into being the responsibility of one group, the government.

By agreement it is the responsibility of each and every one of us.

Our second mistake was to not notice until now the effect on our societies of the combination of this mistake with the emergence of the Information Age. Since we all now have access to nearly all information, it is easy for companies, *without ever directly talking to each other (it is direct collusion that is illegal),* to legally cooperate for self-interest mainly by giving priority to each other's fundamental price increases.

As a result, through mergers and acquisitions all in the corporate community and on Wall Street are now primarily in the business of creating legal duopoly monopolies in every product market.

Corporate leaders now know that if their company is not one of the two pursuing this two other companies will achieve it. So now all companies believe they have no choice but to pursue this in each product market or get out of it.

Most of the public is not yet aware of this "new normal." Therefore, since it is immoral—not fair, those of us who have become aware of it have an obligation to our societies to help everyone else become aware of it.

To assist with this, allow me to point out some familiar product markets where two companies have control of more than 80% of them and, *without ever talking to each other,* are easily able to effect duopoly monopoly behavior. Primarily, they simply match each other's fundamental price increases. They then secondly continuing to compete in price, marketing strategies, efficiencies, reduction of costs, and in every other way:

Coca Cola—Pepsi
CVS—Walgreens
Home Depot—Lowe's
UPS—Fed Ex
Visa—MasterCard
Verizon—AT&T

Google—Apple

Ben & Jerry's—Haagen Dazs

There are many more, also many not easily seen by the public.

I have direct experience of a duopoly monopoly. I am on the board of Ben & Jerry's. We regularly match Haagen Dazs's price increases and they regularly match ours. This is why I am bringing this knowledge to you; this is the new normal. Fortunately, in 2000 when Ben & Jerry's was bought by Unilever we succeeded in signing a legal contract that obligates it to allow us to continue spending the same percentage of our annual budget on social activism as of the year we were bought. So we are now the first "common good corporation" inside a multinational. We give priority in all we do to the common good and second priority to profit for our parent company, Unilever. It, by the way, is the largest ice cream company on Earth. The fact that we are greatly loved, mainly as a result of our aggressive social activism, has had us become its most profitable ice cream product.

The five-year CEO of Unilever, Paul Polman, has observed this combined financial and social success of Ben &Jerry's and now also sees common good business as our future.

Once we were bought this was one of our major agendas. We knew that we needed to become part of a process that matured the multinationals into becoming common good companies. We knew that to save Earth from destroying the ability to support human life we could not have these powerful multinational organizations going in the opposite direction of the rest of us. So this became one of our new missions, beginning with Unilever.

Thus, our Ben & Jerry's board of directors and management has played a part in assisting Unilever to become one of the most aggressive multinationals in unilaterally giving priority to the common good. As I write this they are buying Seventh Generation, which is also based in the same town as Ben & Jerry's, Burlington, VT, for a reported $600 million. They are arranging a similar situation as we have with Unilever. The company will remain separate and independent with Unilever owning the stock. Unilever will provide its efficiencies and wholesale and global distribution systems. The board will remain in existence and by contract be primarily responsible for making sure the company continues to give priority to the common good and second priority to profit. One of the measures will be that it has to continue to be approved as a B-Corp by B-Lab, Inc. which does an evaluation of the socially responsible performance of companies as meeting a high standard.

So there is now a second company operating like Ben & Jerry's, that is, with a legal contract and a board that is responsible for making sure the priority is the common good and the second priority is profitability. This is being done by Polman because he now sees that companies can be more easily and consistently profitable by having the public know this is their priorities. He is also now re-organizing all of Unilever, a $60 billion company with factories in more than half the nations on Earth, to operate in a similar fashion. Every product or product category will have a champion, identify a social purpose, and give priority to the common good and second priority to profitability. Not only that, but he has also been forming relationships with competitors based on this priority, such as working with them to save the rain forests in South America.

This is a maturation of capitalism in the direction of common good capitalism. Paul Polman gets it. Others will surely join him.

This is good news, but a more fundamental question now arises: "How do we, in the Information Age and in a loving way, end this duopoly monopoly system and have all of us, as individuals and organizations, freely choose to keep our agreement to give priority at all times to the common good in a way that cannot be taken advantage of by others?"

I am a Gandhian. Like Mahatma Gandhi, Martin Luther King Jr. and Nelson Mandela, I believe in using love, persuasion, invitation, and non-violent non-cooperation if necessary to have us all understand the importance of correcting this mistake, this economic injustice, this legally allowed crime in our societies.

I also do not see good people and evil people. As when looking at my children, I see less mature and more mature people. Therefore, I see all the people in the corporations as enslaved in an immature system. They are our brothers and sisters. Therefore, we do not want to see them as evil; we want to lovingly liberate them from that system by changing it to one that gives priority to the common good in a way that does not threaten the survival of their companies, jobs, and retirement funds.

We also do not want to end individual freedom and free markets. To do so would be going backwards in maturation. Therefore, we need to build on individual freedom and free markets while still bringing an end to this legally sanctioned breach of our most fundamental agreement with each other.

Thus, in this article I am suggesting that the fundamental part of Bernie's revolution be a common good movement and that his political movement be an extension of it. We can call it a "Common Good Capitalism Movement" or a "Common Good Business Movement" or, to keep it short, just the "Common Good Movement."

The core mission of Bernie Sander's movement is to bring about economic justice. One of the chants at rallies is "We are the 99%!" It exposes the fact that most of the financial benefit of our economy is going to the 1% mainly via the distribution of corporate profits. There is a clear sense in the land, especially among young people, that *our economy is not giving priority to the common good of all* and we have to change it into doing so. The above identifies that one of the main sources of this is the emergence each day of more duopoly monopolies in product markets.

So the question now becomes, "How, *using love, persuasion, invitation, and non-violent action,* do we bring about this now necessary maturation in our economic thinking?"

The following is the strategy around which I believe we will eventually unite.

First, we need to publicly launch a Common Good Movement. Its first goal is to assist all to become aware of the emergence of more legal duopoly monopolies every day. As people become aware of them it will be obvious to more each day that this is immoral, a legal crime we must end.

At that point we will feel trapped. We still want the products the companies produce, but monopoly behavior is not acceptable. We also do not want our rights of individual freedom and free markets to end.

Ultimately, I believe there will be only one solution we will accept because it fulfills all of the above criteria. As indicated above, it is not a new idea.

It is used by every small and large sports league around the world. The competitors meet, agree on the "rules of play," and then secondly compete with referees making sure that in their competitions the common good agreements are consistently sustained as the priority.

In business, in each product market it will be a meeting of the duopoly monopoly companies as well as all the smaller competitors. In direct conversation they will agree upon the common good agreements they will give priority—called the "common good rules of play." Then within them their second priority will be to compete as ferociously as before. Since we now live in the Information Age, this is easily possible.

For instance, in the USA Ben & Jerry's, Haagen Dazs, and the smaller competitors in the super premium ice cream market could meet. There can be some public officials and citizen representatives present without vote so they can afterwards attest that only agreements for the common good were agreed upon. By the way, this is legal; it is direct collusion for self-interest that is not legal.

One of the agreements could be to have the minimum wage in each location be the local living wage. It could be an agreement on wage scales and minimum benefits across all the companies and, where they exist, in full cooperation with labor unions. It could be to use environment-loving packaging. It could be agreements on safety standards. It could even be to annually donate the same percentage of net profits to reduce poverty.

Then instead of referees as in sports competitions they could each publish an annual common good audit by *credible third parties,* the same way they do their financial audits. These "common good referees" will identify the common good agreements and the company's progress on achieving them or timeline for doing so. Going forward this would also allow us, as members of our societies, to be in an on-going public and transparent conversation with the companies on what is best for the common good. As the Civil Rights, Women's, Environment, and Right of Gays to Marry Movements reveal, our understanding of what is best for the common good is constantly maturing.

This would be maturing "capitalism business" into "common good business." It would also be an honoring of our human skill of self-consciousness that allows us to make and keep agreements.

Like all genuinely common good movements, we can now see that what is being requested here is inevitable. It is the only solution to our now duopoly monopoly-dominant marketplace that builds on individual freedom and free markets. We now know that giving priority to profit for a few is immoral—not fair. It can be secondary and fully attended to but to remain a member of our American society it cannot be primary.

No exemptions to giving priority to the common good can be allowed in any society. Doing so, legally or illegally, is a crime.

Also, in our Information Age more than two companies can do this. We are now down to only four major airlines in the US that control more than 80% of the seats: Delta, American, United, and Southwest. They are very adept at matching each other's fundamental price increases and cooperating in many other ways without ever directly coordinating these behaviors with each other. Therefore, the way the Justice Department has dealt with monopoly behavior in the past, the breaking up of companies, will not work. And many duopoly monopolies are multinationals and there is not a global government nor will there be one soon. Thus, it is now also clear that the solution will have to first occur in the private sector, as voluntary common good behavior.

Our Information Age allows us to organize all the competitors in each product market into the equivalent of a soccer league. And new teams, that is, new competitors, are always free to join the league. And if they do not join the league to attempt to take advantage of immoral behaviors, they can now easily be publicly exposed as doing so which can lead to economic failure and eventually, perhaps, laws that will not allow it.

This way everyone wins.

Relative to one another, it will not cost the companies a penny. Where appropriate they can at the same time raise their costs and still secondly compete on price, packaging, marketing, and, like Ben & Jerry's, the development of a love for the company by the public.

But no longer will it be at the expense of the employees, community, or environment. Allow me to repeat that: no longer will it be at the expense of the employees, community, or environment.

In addition, these usually multinational companies will be experienced as valued partners in building more mature societies.

By the way, this direct cooperation for the common good can also take place at the local level. For instance, all the restaurants in town could agree on a minimum wage for kitchen employees.

Finally, as with all common good movements, those on both the political right and left will eventually join us. Just as all babies are now born into societies that know the Earth is round there will be a day when all babies are born into societies that agree we need to very self-consciously together manage Earth for sustainability. They will also eventually be born into societies that know that all individuals and organizations within them have agreed to give priority to the common good and no exceptions are allowed.

Those on the political right will particularly like that it is a private sector solution. And those on the political left will like that the freely chosen priority is the common good and the process is open and transparent. However, this solution is not on the political right or left. It is beyond the fundamental polarization between the two and into a more mature business community, *a common good business community.* It is where the freely chosen priority is the common good, agreements with competitors that honor this priority are made in direct face-to-face meetings, and the on-going process is a voluntary open and transparent monitoring of their behavior so all are accountable to the public for sustaining as the priority the freely chosen agreements made that give priority to the common good.

There is no paternalism in this solution: the companies having to take orders from a government or any other agent. In the private sector, this is solely the result of the freely chosen individual actions of the companies. It is also the overt honoring of our most fundamental agreement with each other as societies, now an Earth society.

When common good business is in every sector, the result will be that economically we will finally feel we are all in this together.

Corporate leaders, have your company be one of the first to declare your support for the Common Good Movement. It is the inevitable future because we have matured to where we now know it is immoral—not fair—to give priority in a society to anything other than the common good. Also, be one of the first to arrange the above described meeting with all of your competitors.

Like Mahatma Gandhi, Martin Luther King Jr. and Nelson Mandela, we want our economic justice movement to be both a common good and political movement. Legislation in support of common good business will eventually be passed.

However, without it being based on the credibility of a common good movement embraced by the vast majority of Americans, policies in support of it will not easily come to a vote and be passed.

In the short term, we may or may not have full success with the legislative efforts of our political movement. *However, in the long run we know our common good movement will be successful.* We are constantly maturing. And we are constantly correcting our mistakes. And we are also constantly correcting for the changes in context such as the emergence of the Information Age. Also, this will eventually result in legislation in support of it.

As Nelson Mandela said, "love comes…naturally to the human heart."

If so, common good business is the natural next layer of maturity after capitalism business.

Please go to our website and consider joining our movement by adding your name and organizations to the list of supporters. Also, get in touch with us if you want to do some actions in your community in support of it, such as launching a local chapter anywhere in the world (go to *About Us/Guidelines for Starting a Common Good Chapter*):

www.commongoodcapitalism.org.

And if you want to read more about the arguments for this movement, I have written a book entitled *Common Good Capitalism Is Inevitable*, available on Amazon.

Here is one action currently being considered and anyone can organize a local Common Good Capitalism Movement chapter and take such an action at the annual meeting of a duopoly monopoly company in his or her area.

To in a fun and loving way raise awareness of us all of the existence of duopoly monopolies we invite many people, perhaps hundreds, perhaps thousands, to the parking lot outside the hotel where duopoly companies are holding their annual meeting of shareholders, for instance Home Depot's meeting in Atlanta. We can request that someone from the company come outside and receive a trophy for having achieved in home improvement a duopoly monopoly with Lowe's. We can then pull back a curtain and show them an even bigger trophy they will receive when they join with Lowe's and their other competitors and reach some agreements, any agreements that give priority to the common good, and have those agreements monitored by each providing to the public annual common good audits.

To ultimately be successful at the depth he and his supporters seek, Bernie's "economic justice revolution" needs to be based on a common good movement. My suggestion is that it be the above described Common Good Movement.

The above editorial begs the question, "Why would the people on Wall Street and in corporate America take advantage of a legal crime rather than honor the fundamental agreement of us all in any human society to give priority to the common good?"

The short answer is that they have not reached full maturity in the skill of self-consciousness. They are still operating as if one of the lower five layers is the highest layer.

Like any skill, there are layers of smaller skills we master that build on one another and can as habits accumulate into the full skill. An example is the skill of riding a bicycle. We first learn to push off and jump onto the seat without falling down. Next we learn to stay on it and pedal without falling off. Next we learn to turn it without falling off. Each smaller skill becomes a habit and builds on the one before it in a natural progression toward the mastery of the full skill.

However, without a tradition of eldering our children up the mastery of the smaller skills of all seven layers to achieve full maturity in the *skill* of self-consciousness, we become stuck at one of the middle layers the rest of their lives. If ignorant of the existence of the higher layers, or even that there are seven smaller skills to learn, we will believe that whichever layer we have achieved is the highest layer. While growing up we need to at least be aware of the need to master the skills of all seven layers to achieve full maturity in this skill.

Here is one of the most important insights in this book: if stuck at one of the first five layers as if it is the highest layer, it is natural to give priority to the self-interest of our physical bodies. Without wise eldering we naturally assume this while mastering the smaller skills of the first five layers. It is part of the process of learning a language and becoming self-conscious.

The seven layers of maturity of the skill of self-consciousness will be fully described in *Chapter 4: Mastering the Skill of Self-Consciousness*. However, I will soon briefly describe them in this *Introduction*.

We will probably all agree on the first five layers. This is because nearly all reading this book already know these smaller skills. We have matured as individuals and societies to where they are now common knowledge. Nearly everyone knows them and it is assumed that we will honor them in all our relationships with each other.

Before I describe them, it is important to note that they are *skills*.

There is only one correct way to do a skill.

However, there are many ways to not do it correctly. Learning a skill is not in the place of "I have to be free to do it anyway I want." There is only one correct way to walk instead of crawling. There is only one correct way to remain balanced on a bicycle. There is only one correct way to drive an automobile. This is why I am confident you will agree on the first five. You already know these smaller skills and know the one and only way to do each. Therefore, since most of us in our developed societies already know them, they are common knowledge.

However, the last two smaller skills of the skill of self-consciousness are not common knowledge.

So there could be disagreement on what they are. Since they are smaller skills that we can only learn in relationship with direct experience, we will eventually come to agree on what they are. They are skills where there is only one way to do each. Therefore, we will eventually also turn them into agreed upon common knowledge.

In this book I will argue that it is easy and obvious to identify both of them in our direct experience. *However, someone has to at least point them out to each person because they are not yet common knowledge.* The wonderful thing about nature that can have us be comfortably optimistic is that, since they are skills we can all learn, we know that someday they will be common knowledge.

Secondly, I will argue that it is ignorance of knowing and mastering the smaller skills of the last two layers that explains why people on Wall Street and in corporate America are comfortable joining forces to cease an opportunity to take advantage of legal crimes when they can. As mentioned above, without wise eldering while growing up, at least having our children know there are seven layers of smaller skills to learn to achieve full maturity in the skill of self-consciousness, at the five lower layers of maturity in this skill it is natural to assume our highest priority is the self-interest of our physical bodies.

Here is the main reason this is the case.

Without the guidance of respected elders who are fully mature in this skill, during the learning and mastery of the first five layers we are still unconsciously operating on the false assumption about reality it was necessary to assume to create, learn, or use a human language. That inaccurate assumption is that the universe is an immense number of separate parts.

The universe, as I will guide you into directly experiencing in a few pages, is an indivisible whole. However, to create a human language it was necessary to assume it is an immense number of separate parts so we can give each one of them a name. This allows us to talk about them with each other and ourselves. It also allows us to become self-conscious, to identify the relationships between and among them. It also allows us to know what we are doing while we are doing it, talk about the past, plan for the future, and consistently execute the plan in the present.

It is only in the mastery of the smaller skills of the last two layers of maturity of the skill of self-consciousness that we realize this assumption of separate parts is false. At the same time, it is necessary to assume it to create, learn, or use a human language as a *skill*. In turn, it is this that allows us to be self-conscious. So this false assumption about reality is a valuable *tool*.

However, it is a valuable mutually agreed upon illusion tool.

Over the last many decades, scientists assumed our skill of self-consciousness was the result of something biological in our brains. We now know it is a *skill* we learn as a result of the creation of this mutually agreed upon illusion tool.

By the way, thousands of years ago, before there was the existence of human languages, how could two people have agreed to use the sound "cup" to represent a cup and, thereby, have created the first word of a human language? We now know the only way they could have done it. They both put their hands on top of each other on a cup type object, looked each other in the eyes, and when they said the word "cup" to each other they had the eyes-to-eyes experience together of peace (local oneness) instead of the experience of conflict (separate and competing parts).

They recognized this mutual experience of peace as the experience of agreement (the experience of local oneness).

We still do this to this day. When we reach an agreement with another we look into each other's eyes and recognize together the mutual experience of peace (local oneness) instead of the *mutual experience of conflict (separate and competing parts).*

The creation of a human language is a skill, and like any skill there is only one way to do it. There can be many languages. However, this or something similar to it is the only way this first word of a language could have come into existence. As Tom Wolfe describes in the form of a story in his recent best-selling book about the path of the scientists to get to this conclusion, *The Kingdom of Speech*, it is the discovery and utilization of this *skill* that has raised the human species to a level of skill above the rest of the animal kingdom.

Briefly, here is a description of the smaller skills of the first five layers of maturity of self-consciousness that are now part of our common knowledge. The names I have given them are Baby, Toddler, Child, Teen, and Adult.

As a baby we learn to *respond to our sensations.* As a toddler we learn to *respond to differences:* mommy or no mommy, milk or no milk, and most important, happy (oneness experience) or not happy (separate and competing parts experience). As a child we learn a human language. Now our priority is no longer our sensations or responding to differences. It is our *wants.* We are over here, the candy is on the table, we want it, but we can only go get some if our parents allow it.

In learning a human language at this early development of our brains, we naturally and unconsciously also accept the fundamental assumption about reality in language that the universe is an immense number of separate parts, like the words in a language.

As a teen our brains are developed to where we can discover we have the *ability and skill of free choice.* Instead of only responding to multiple-choice options presented by our parents and others we can create our own multiple-choice options. If mom asks if we want chocolate, vanilla, or strawberry ice cream, we can respond by saying, "I don't want to talk about ice cream. I want to talk about getting a car."

At the adult layer, the fifth layer, we discover our most important free choice is our *fundamental belief.* We also realize we have been unconsciously operating on the many beliefs we inherited through our upbringing. We now want to freely choose a fundamental belief because it will provide us the pleasure of self-consciously experiencing our lives as meaningful. At all times there will be a reason for doing one thing rather than another. Now *honoring our fundamental belief* becomes our priority in all we do. Our lives are now not only meaningful but, as a result, more enjoyable.

In fact, the reason we always fully learn and turn into a habit the smaller skill of each next layer is because living our lives is always a more enjoyable experience.

We choose our fundamental belief from the smorgasbord of beliefs we come upon. Of course, our fundamental belief can mature as our thinking matures. Initially it is usually that it makes sense to always give priority to whatever we want, the self-interests of our physical bodies. As the result of learning a language without wise eldering, that has been our *unconscious fundamental belief* since being a child. However usually we discover that is immature and we want a fundamental belief that deals with the ability and rights of others to also seek what they want. Most people end up choosing a religious or philosophical belief, anything from Christianity to Islam to capitalism to socialism to democracy to science to something they formulate on their own such as to "love thy neighbor as thyself."

I think most readers will agree that these are the smaller skills of the first five layers of the skill of self-consciousness. I think we can also easily agree that most of the people in the USA are operating as if one of the last three is the highest layer: the child layer (wants are the priority), teen layer (free choice is the priority), or adult layer (a fundamental belief is the priority). I think we can also easily agree that few people in the USA think of this within a framework of layers of maturity of the skill of self-consciousness. *Thus, they are unaware of which layer they are giving priority within such a framework.* Finally, I think we can then also agree that our society's decisions give priority to each of these at different times without much discussion or awareness that each is a layer of maturity of the skill of self-consciousness.

It is only at the next layer of maturity, the sixth layer I have labeled the "Elder Layer," that we discover we have been operating on the assumption about reality present in human languages. It is that the universe is an immense number of separate parts. At the sixth layer we discover that the structure of the universe is the exact opposite. It is an indivisible whole.

Watch out! Don't agree or disagree it is this. As we did at the adult layer, that would be giving our power to another *outside belief*, a belief chosen from the smorgasbord of beliefs we have come upon. An *inside belief* is one that is the result of discovering a fact in direct experience. It is always secondary in importance to the fact we can affirm it is accurate in any moment *by turning our attention again to our direct experience.*

This is keeping our power. Since from the inside each of us is the only one who can mover our arms and legs and think our thoughts and act on them, it is essential that we each keep our power.

Instead, join me below in taking a few minutes now to put aside all your beliefs, *keep your power instead of giving it to an outside belief*, and use it to study your immediate and direct experience to see if this is, indeed, the accurate fundamental fact we can actually discover to be accurate at any time in our direct experience with nature.

Knowing anything in direct experience has it become knowledge we can no longer deny we know. It then naturally and effortlessly becomes a knowledge skill. It is no longer an outside belief (a bunch of mutually agreed upon illusions) to which we are giving our power. Once it is a skill it is secondly a belief, an inside belief.

It is a way of representing it in words so we can talk about it with others and ourselves. This, by the way, is true freedom. When at the Adult Layer we choose an outside belief, regardless of its content, we are giving our power to a second thing, the outside belief. What we usually fail to notice is that now our second priority is to *obey* it. Thus we think we are in full freedom because we freely chose it. However, we are really in partial freedom in the illusion we are in full freedom.

We only achieve full freedom when our most fundamental belief is an inside belief as a result of discovering it is true in direct right-now-experi-

ence. Then it naturally and effortlessly becomes primarily a skill rather than primarily an outside belief.

Therefore, the mutually agreed upon assumption that allowed us the ability to create and use our human languages and thereby be self-conscious is a *mutually agreed upon illusion tool.* An extremely valuable tool, but still a mutually agreed upon illusion tool. There are more than 6,000 languages on Earth. Each is a mutually agreed upon illusion tool.

Below is one of the main ways people throughout history have discovered the knowledge skill of the Elder Layer. They studied their breath. In a few paragraphs, I will guide you into discovering this knowledge skill by doing that.

First, fundamentally there are two kinds of skills: experience skills and knowledge skills. Walking and riding a bicycle are experience skills. They can be solely learned in direct experience. Knowing that the best way to walk through a wall is where there is a door is a knowledge skill. Knowing the Earth is round even though it appears flat when chopping vegetables or building a house is a knowledge skill. The smaller skills of the last two layers of maturity of the skill of self-consciousness are knowledge skills. They are, of course, confirmed as accurate in direct experience. However, once confirmed as accurate there, *they are primarily utilized as knowledge skills in our thinking.*

For you to become a participant in easily and enjoyably leading us into our maturation into common good capitalism, it will be necessary for you to have matured into having the knowledge and skill of the sixth layer. It is where you have discovered *in direct experience,* not primarily from agreeing with some words, that the universe is an indivisible whole. When we discover something to be true in direct experience, it naturally and effortlessly becomes a skill, a knowledge skill, rather than only an experience skill or a belief in words.

It also eventually becomes a habit, part of who you are.

So it is essential that you discover that the universe is an indivisible whole from a study of your right-now-experience. Therefore, let me now guide you into having the direct experience of the oneness of nature.

For a few moments, put all your current beliefs aside. This will allow you to turn your attention to your breathing to discover what is the most fundamental fact about life, and have it become a knowledge skill, solely from studying your direct right-now-experience.

We have been breathing since birth and will be breathing until we die. We are not self-consciously choosing to breathe. It is happening naturally and effortlessly. So the question becomes, "Who or what is doing our breathing?"

It is obvious that if we took our lungs out of our physical bodies and put them on a table we would not be able to breathe. Thus, we need our physical bodies to be alive and our lungs in them for us to breathe. So it is more accurate to say, "Our lungs and physical bodies are doing our breathing."

It next becomes clear that without the air that is always surrounding us we would not be able to breathe. So it becomes more accurate to say, "Our lungs, our physical bodies, and the air are doing our breathing."

We then realize that if the Earth did not have its atmosphere but instead had the atmosphere of Mars, we would not be able to breathe. So it is more accurate to say, "Our lungs, our physical bodies, the air, and the Earth's atmosphere are doing our breathing."

And if the Earth is not in the particular relationship with the rest of the universe that allows it to have its atmosphere, if it had the relationship of Mars or Venus, we would not be able to breathe. At this point in our study of our direct experience we discover it is most accurate to say, "Our lungs, physical bodies, the air, the Earth's atmosphere, and the universe are doing our breathing," or more simply "The universe is doing our breathing."

It then also becomes clear that if any one of these parts were not present and always doing exactly what each is doing the universe would not be able to do our breathing.

Thus, through this study of our breathing in our right-now-experience with nature it is obvious that the universe is an indivisible whole.

This is one of the ways this most fundamental truth has been discovered throughout history. If you focused on your direct experience while you were doing the above, you have now discovered it there. Like any other truth discovered from a study of direct experience, you will never be able to fool yourself into thinking you do not know it. As a result, it is now knowledge you possess. Therefore, it will now naturally and effortlessly begin to become a knowledge skill and habit and used in all of your thinking. There are other knowledge skills you will need to learn to have this consistently be visible in your thinking and behavior. However, you will now naturally and effortlessly be in a search to find them.

We also now know that the assumption about reality we have probably been operating on since learning a human language is false. The universe is not an immense number of separate parts. That assumption is part of the mutually agreed upon illusion tool called "human language."

Therefore, our accurate self-definition is "we are each first the indivisible universe and secondly our physical bodies."

Our physical body is the only part of the universe over which we have sole and complete inside control. However, that does not make us separate from everything else. That is just an ability our part has, just as water has wetting ability, clouds have rain ability, trees have the ability to create fruit, and dogs have the ability to bark. The different parts of the indivisible universe have different abilities but that does not make them separate from one another anymore than our hand having a different ability than our nose are experienced as *primarily* separate from one another.

We first experience all the parts of our physical bodies as our entire body and only secondly as parts. If we are in an automobile accident and we need our leg amputated, we give priority to the good of the whole body and second priority to keeping the leg and let it be amputated.

In our thinking we are always first our whole physical body and only secondly any one of its parts.

Now this priority way of thinking of the different parts of our physical bodies, as first the whole body and secondly any of its parts, is now the way we also think about the universe: we are first the indivisible universe and secondly our physical body parts of it.

As will be described later in this book, this priority pattern of thinking, the pattern of thinking we are always using when thinking about the inside of our skin, is the pattern of thinking that represents the oneness of nature. At the last two layers we learn the importance of always giving it priority *while also using* the separate parts pattern of thinking that allows us to be self-conscious. By the way, throughout history the priority pattern of thinking has been used to define moral behavior: freely choosing to give *priority* to the common good.

At this sixth layer, we also become aware that there is no evidence that the universe will ever die while it is obvious that we will each die. This makes it easy to freely choose to give priority to being the universe and second priority to being our physical bodies. Our true self-interest is now the self-interest of the universe.

Thus, what we have labeled "moral behavior" is a natural layer of maturity in the skill of self-consciousness. It is the sixth layer.

The mastery of the seventh and final layer, what I have labeled the "Mature Elder Layer," also has to do with our relationship with human language. At the seventh layer, we realize that we are still giving priority to words, the *belief* that the universe is an indivisible whole. Words are a bunch of mutually agreed upon illusions. They are in the illusion of separate parts. We now know that in reality there is not a second thing to receive our power.

We are then left with the question, "What do I now give priority that is not a second thing like a belief?" We eventually discover there is only one thing that does this: giving priority to experience. We realize that we want to keep using a human language because it allows us to be self-conscious; but, *while doing both simultaneously,* we have to give priority each moment to direct experience, the experience of being the universe. Just as we primarily relate with our physical body as an experience, we now primarily relate with the entire universe as an experience. We now know that the entire universe is our physical body and, therefore, our true self-interest is the common good of it all as an indivisible whole. Experience has no boundaries.

We discover that what is most important is not the size of the universe but this oneness relationship with it.

There are other smaller skills to master to turn these last two layers of maturity of the skill of self-consciousness into habits. They will be described in *Chapter 4: Mastering the Skill of Self-Consciousness.*

If the knowledge and skills of all seven layers was common knowledge in our American society, we would make sure our children were well eldered into the mastery in the smaller skills of all seven layers before they leave home, and particularly before they marry. We would do it as thoroughly as we make sure they have mastered the smaller skills of the first five layers. This eldering activity would also be the highest priority in our societies—global, national, and local. We would know there is nothing that is more important for the health *and* happiness of each child and our societies than this.

The key to discovering the smaller skills of the last two layers of maturity in the skill of self-consciousness is understanding the relationship between our human languages and the reality that the universe is an indivisible whole.

The creation of our human languages was only possible by creating as a tool the mutually agreed upon illusion that the universe is an immense number of separate parts. This, in turn, allows us to be self-conscious parts of it, to talk about the parts with each other and ourselves. However, and as described earlier, without wise eldering we can become stuck at assuming one of the first five layers is the highest layer. We would not know from a young age there are seven layers of smaller skills to learn. We would then unconsciously—without knowing we are doing it—assume that the highest layer we know is the highest layer. We will be giving priority to our sensations, differences, wants, right to free choice, or our freely chosen fundamental belief. Or we would be giving priority to different one's of these at different times.

Growing up without the presence of respected elders artfully eldering us has a serious effect on individuals and societies. Especially if all around us are also operating as if one of the first five is the highest layer, we could easily get stuck in the assumption that one of them is the highest layer. Our behavior would then be in ignorance of the fact that the universe is an indivisible whole. As a result, we would naturally assume we are each only our physical body, the only part of the universe where from the inside we have sole and complete control. Today, many are still assuming they are each only their physical body.

This also has us assume competition is the fundamental process in nature: each part is a separate part giving priority to its self-interest in relationship with all the other parts in a consistent fight for survival. As you will see as you read further, if the universe is an indivisible whole—which I hope you just had the direct experience of this being a fact, then cooperation is the fundamental process in nature. Competition is a lower form of cooperation: it is not possible without an agreement that what is being competed over is wanted by both people. That agreement is the *cooperative context* that is always present for competition to occur. Compromise, agreement, and love are the more mature forms of cooperation than competition. If the universe is an indivisible whole, we can't escape always fundamentally cooperating.

Thus, whether or not it has the skill of self-consciousness, each part is naturally and effortlessly giving priority to what is best for the indivisible whole. This is each part's true self-interest. Evolution is the result of each part cooperating, albeit at different layers of maturity of the skill of cooperation, for the common good. It is not "the survival of the fittest through competition." The latter conclusion was within the illusion that there are separate parts and it is possible for competition to exist outside of a cooperative context.

You will also eventually discover that *maturation* is the particular kind of cooperation that is the fundamental process in nature. Cooperation is a process. It does not reveal why the process is occurring. Maturation is why the process of cooperation is occurring. We are going somewhere. Not primarily in the world of the illusion of separate parts (time and space); but in maturation. We are becoming more of what we, the universe, can become.

Lastly, this has been a description of the layers of maturity of the *skill* of self-consciousness. Above this we can give priority to any belief, which we will call a "super belief." Any religious, philosophical, scientific, or other belief can be our priority, our super belief. For instance, it could be that Abraham and Moses have provided us the truths to guide our lives, Jesus is the Son of God, Mohammad is God's Messenger, all who have died are still present in another dimension, or science will ultimately answer all questions. Herein I am solely describing the skill of self-consciousness. Anyone can give priority to their super belief and second priority to the use of this skill.

Over the last centuries we have been living at the adult layer. Relationships, both individual and social, have been a clash of *outside beliefs,* for instance the divine right of kings verses democracy, capitalism verses communism, and Sunni Islam verses Shiite Islam. We are now ready to graduate into the skills of the Elder and Mature Elder Layers.

In the years leading up to 2008 some people on Wall Street discovered how to take advantage of a legal crime. Since the public was operating on the assumption that home mortgages are nearly always paid, they arranged for people not financially qualified to acquire many mortgages. They could then package them into securities to sell to investors, thereby making a large profit. No one went to jail for doing this because they discovered a way to commit a legal crime. It caused a deep global depression that resulted in much suffering for billions of people.

In my judgment, as a human species we are in the process of maturing into the Elder Layer. This will result in many changes in the way we live our lives together.

Parenting will be giving priority to eldering our children to full maturity in the skill of self-consciousness before they are in their twenties and definitely before they marry. To better succeed in accomplishing this, as well as for the fun of it, friends will form into communities, a re-villaging of our lives.

It will enable us to manage Earth for sustainability. It will lead us to create a forever-growing trust fund for the poor, invest it in our common good corporations so they are participating in ending poverty, and use the annual profits to provide a minimum income for more of them each year until there are no longer poor people. Then use the annual profits for the common good in other ways.

Common good democracies will emerge as *parallel governance systems* with no legal power but with the greatest power because they will work over time toward a near consensus on issues: at least a 70% vote of the representatives from the for-profit and non-profit organizations in the community. As a result, no one will be able to be elected to office who does not support the community's near consensus on issues. Also, the members of the community will now have a way to discuss the issues and reach agreements rather than only being caught up in the candidates' horse race.

Common good nations will emerge defined *by agreement rather than geography*. Anyone on Earth can at any time join or leave them and, while equally valuing both, people will give priority to these freely chosen nations over their geographically defined nations. This will have the latter eventually become very secondary and wars be reduced as a result of members of these nations-by-agreement living on all geographies.

Finally, to the surprise of many, eventually our multinational corporations will increasingly take a lead to make our world a better place, initially in the operations of their common good businesses. They will also eventually work with governments, international agencies, and non-profits to establish labor, environmental, and community standards, and eventually legislation in each nation, that give priority to the common good. They will even eventually compete for the support of the public in a new way: by doing extracurricular activities such as building modern environmentally aware towns in poor countries and training the local citizens to manage them before they leave.

A further development of each of these ideas will be presented in *Chapter 7: Some of Us Are Ready to Mature Ourselves and Our Societies into the Elder and Mature Elder Layers of Maturity.*

In our corporate community, primarily cooperating is already *quietly and indirectly* happening. As a result of our easy and quick access to nearly all information, there is nothing that will stop it no matter how many competitors in each product area. In the marketplace duopoly, triopoly, quadropoly, or whatever duopolies will continue to emerge and shrink in number. As in sports leagues, whether a local children's soccer league or the National Basketball Association (NBA), we always prefer freely chosen agreements as the container within which the competition occurs. Therefore, becoming the equivalent of a sports league and giving priority to direct and transparent cooperation for the common good will eventually happen. The public will then continuously support this free market maturation into common good capitalism.

Sadly, but naturally, our governments will always be reacting to new legal crimes until people and societies mature into the final two layers of maturity of the skill of self-consciousness. Then people will naturally, effortlessly, and joyfully give priority to the common good, the maturation of the universe. Particularly in the Information Age, no paternalistic system will fully succeed at stopping legal crimes before they are found and executed. And people operating at the lower five layers in ignorance of the highest two layers will always be searching to find them. They will only be shamed or educated into the wisdom of not doing so when most of the people around them are operating at the higher layers of maturity of the skill of self-consciousness.

All of this will be thoroughly described as you read further. However, in summary, since maturation is the fundamental process in nature, human beings and their societies will eventually mature into the skills of the last two layers of maturity of the skill of self-consciousness. They will then become common knowledge. Therefore, I am comfortable predicting that its economic expression, herein labeled "common good capitalism," is inevitable.

1
Davos

CAN THE CURRENT CEOs OF SOME OF OUR LARGEST MULTINA-
tional corporations, leading economists, Wall Street professionals, and presidents of our business schools mature into giving priority to the common
good? If it is natural for us to mature in our skill of self-consciousness to
where we freely make this choice, then, like us all, I believe they want to
find a way to give priority to the common good in their daily lives at work.

In 2013 I had an opportunity to test this belief during conversations
with many of the top chief executives in the world at the annual World
Economic Forum in Davos, Switzerland. I ended up sharing my thoughts
with many of them, including some of the most recognizable names in the
business world. They included Mike Duke, CEO of Walmart; Jamie Dimon,
CEO of J.P. Morgan; Indra Nooyi, CEO of Pepsi; former U.S. Secretary of
the Treasury Larry Summers; Muhammad Yunus, founder of Grameen
Bank and winner of the 2006 Nobel Peace Prize; Wendell Brown, CEO of
Appeo and Silicon Valley entrepreneur; Ray Suarez, video journalist with
PBS; Jack DeGioia, president of Georgetown University; David Gergen,
consultant to several U.S. Presidents; Drew Gilpin Faust, president of Har-
vard University; Kenneth Rogoff, economist at Harvard University; Joseph
Stiglitz, economist and recipient of the Nobel Memorial Prize in Economic
Sciences; and Xiang Bing, president of the largest business school in China.

I was usually introduced as a founder of the Calvert Social Funds and
member of the board of Ben & Jerry's. Once introductions were done I
seized the opportunity to request of each of them if I could ask a question.
They all said yes.

I then stated that I was aware that the highest priority of multinational
corporations is to become number one or two in each product market. They
all indicated that they knew this was true.

What was important about stating this in the beginning is that it revealed that I was part of this very private conversation within the corporate community. It is a conversation they usually avoid bringing up with

the public or press. However by comfortably stating it as the fundamental construct of the question I was about to ask I was immediately perceived as being a member of the inside team, not against the corporate community. Since both the Calvert Social Funds and Ben & Jerry's are progressive companies, it was essential that I reveal to them that I was aware of this silent priority within our community.

Next I stated, "This will only become more extensive and at some point the public will become aware of it. The political left and right will then call it a monopoly with another face.

"The question will then become, 'How do duopolies protect their duopolies?'"

This question was always met with silence and glassy eyes—and keen attention to what I would say next. Solely in my judgment from the expressions on their faces, I do not think any of them had ever asked themselves this question. This is understandable. Much of the merger and acquisition activity has been focused on becoming a duopoly in each product market and not bringing attention to it in the hopes it is never noticed. Since it is legal they are aware that if they don't do it another two companies will so they have no choice.

Then, after giving each a moment to realize they had never asked themselves this question, I continued speaking before they could change the direction of the conversation, "In my judgment there is only one thing the public will respect. The two companies will need to voluntarily and directly reach agreements to raise for the common good the level of the labor, environmental, and social playing field while fully continuing to compete as their second priority."

Every person, and this is not an exaggeration, expressed some words affirming complete and enthusiastic agreement with that answer. I had not only provided the logical and natural answer to the question, but it was also a positive for the duopolies. When the presence of duopoly monopolies is widely noticed by the public, this new priority also might allow their duopolies to survive. So there was clearly nothing to dislike.

The only person who initially disagreed with me was Jamie Dimon, the CEO of J.P. Morgan and one of the most powerful people on Wall Street. He said cooperation would be illegal and began to walk away. I turned to him and said, "You know there is a way for it to be legal. It is cooperation for the common good, not collusion for self-interests." He turned and said calmly and smiling broadly, "You are right."

Most were interested in hearing more, so I provided an example of a business I know: ice cream. Ben & Jerry's and Häagen Dazs control 82 percent of the super premium ice cream market in the United States and we have expanded into mostly the same thirty-five nations. Ben & Jerry's is now owned by Unilever. Its CEO, Paul Polman, who many of the executives indicated they knew, is a progressive. So we could pilot this idea with Ben & Jerry's and Häagen Dazs, owned by Nestlé. Both companies could agree to raise the minimum wage where our ice creams are produced to be the livable wage in each area. Everyone wins. Relative to one another it would not cost the companies a penny: they can equally raise the price. The employees win and the community wins. The smaller competitors would eventually choose to join in the agreement rather than be attacked by the press or be exposed by the transparency of the Internet. The governments will love it because it is cooperation for the common good (legal), not collusion. And the duopolies will be seen as good guys who are cooperating to make the world a better place. Of course, they will also be sustaining the existence of their duopoly positions.

I would then further point out that there is no global government or union but there are global corporations. This will provide them the opportunity to take the lead to make the world a better place for us all, to end the race to the bottom in the use of people, natural resources, and communities, and to instead lead in the rise of all from the bottom. I also pointed out that I believe the first duopolies to market with this approach, like Ben & Jerry's, which already unilaterally gives priority to the common good including having our minimum wage be the livable wage, will become the most loved brand names, and that would be smart marketing.

What was most interesting to me was that not a single person gave any indication he or she had thought of this as a possible future. Yet when presented with it as the logical solution to a serious problem they had not yet anticipated, but would definitely some day have to confront, they fully supported the logical solution I presented to them.

Hence the reason why I am reporting these conversations to you at the beginning of this book. What I described to them is not only a possible future. In my judgment it is the most likely future and is eventually inevitable.

Common Good Capitalism *is just a matter of time and a maturation of the thinking, not just of them, but eventually of us all.*

As I will describe in detail later, I now believe that cooperation is the fundamental process in nature, not competition as so many of us were taught. Not only that, but a certain kind of cooperation is the fundamental process in nature: maturation. Once we learn to execute a skill at a more mature layer it becomes a habit and we do not go back to executing it at the less mature layer at which we had previously been executing it. As mentioned earlier and are obvious examples, once we learned to walk we did not go back to primarily crawling to get around. Once we learned to ride a bicycle, we no longer easily fell off of it. Once we learned to use chopsticks, we no longer used them with two hands. Once we mastered the skill of operating our societies as democracies, we did not revert back to dictatorships. Maturation is the fundamental process in nature and it cannot be stopped.

Self-consciousness is also a skill.

As we master a particular layer but remain ignorant of the higher ones, we naturally assume it is the highest layer. A child's priority is getting what he or she wants (Child Layer) with no awareness that at some point in the future his or her brain will mature to where exercising the ability and right of *free choice* will be more important (Teen Layer). Or, later, living according to his or her *freely chosen fundamental belief* will be more important than free choice (Adult Layer). That is, our priority each moment is defined by the highest layer of maturity of the skill of self-consciousness we know until we discover the next higher layer. Then we naturally, effortlessly, and fully embrace it and, as we did with the skill of each lower layer, also turn it into a habit.

The discovery of each layer increases our ability to cooperate with all that is around us to directly participate in the maturation of our friends, our lovers, our children, and our societies, that is, of the universe from wherever we are standing. This increases the experience of the joy of happiness in our lives. So when it is discovered we naturally fully embrace each next layer of maturity in the skill of self-consciousness.

This process of discovering the smaller skill of each next layer in the natural progression continues until we discover and master the smaller skill of the highest layer (Mature Elder Layer). As with riding a bicycle or using chopsticks, there is a highest layer and when mastered it is obvious there is a not a higher layer.

We could get more proficient at each smaller skill, but there is not a higher layer of maturity to learn to execute the total basic skill.

As mentioned earlier, throughout history it has been discovered that at the highest layer of the human skill of self-consciousness we freely choose to give priority to the common good of us all, called "moral behavior," "enlightenment," and "the state of grace" to present, as we did earlier, a few terms and phrases that are used to label this behavior. Secondly, it is natural for each of us to mature to full maturity in the skill of self-consciousness. When discovered, we naturally, effortlessly, and freely choose to embrace the smaller skill of each next layer of maturity in the progression because it allows us to experience more joy in our lives.

However, in the absence of being reared in a community that is aware of the layers and of the importance of having us learn them, we can become unconsciously stuck at one of the lower layers and therefore ignorant of the existence of the higher layers. We would continue to operate believing we are at the highest layer.

In addition, if everyone in our community and wider society are also operating as if a particular layer is the highest layer, our entire society can be stuck at that layer for generations. As you will see when you read further, I think that is our current situation on Earth.

One of the purposes of this book is for more of us to become aware of our current layer of maturation and for each of us to then complete the process of mastering the remaining layers to achieve full maturity in the basic skill of self-consciousness.

No one can do this for us.

As parents we can guide our children into the mastery of the early layers of maturity of this skill. However, once we discover and master the teenage layer of maturity, where our ability and right of individual freedom is discovered, from that point forward the discovery and mastery of the smaller skills of the remaining layers can only be the result of free choice. Like learning the smaller skills that accumulate into the total skill of riding a bicycle, each of the layers builds on the one before it and does not end the smaller skills of any of the lower layers. Instead they are each turned into habits and sustained as essential parts of the skill of the next layer we are learning.

So once the teenage layer has been discovered each next layer can only be the result of free choice. Mature Elder parents know this and, therefore, do a good job all along of educating their children that there are layers of maturity of the human skill of self-consciousness, there is a highest layer, and they can only be learned in the natural progression

Thus, this book presents the argument that when the higher layers of the skill of self-consciousness are widely discovered and mastered, the result will be a widespread maturation in our economic activity into common good capitalism. The most fundamental guiding principle of capitalism is a respect for individual freedom and free markets. When operating at the higher layers of maturity in the human skill of self-consciousness, we *freely choose* to give priority to the common good of us all.

This will not be the result of revolution. As I think you will come to agree, it will be the result of the maturation of some of us in the beginning but eventually of us all into the Elder Layer of the skill of self-consciousness.

In the conversations with the above people who allowed me to go further, I pointed out that cooperation, not competition, is the fundamental process in nature and that I can quickly and easily demonstrate that this is true.

Sticking my hand out as if I were holding an apple, I said, "If I have an apple in my hand and neither you nor I want it, anyone could take it and we would both be as happy afterwards as before. However, if you want it and I want it, we could compete over it."

Then with emphasis I said, "*Note this: the competition can only take place if there is agreement that who gets the apple is important. That agreement is the cooperative context. Competition is not possible outside of a cooperative context.*"

I then continued, "Through a simple example such as this it is obvious that cooperation, not competition, is the fundamental process in nature. Anytime two people agree to do anything, from meeting to have a cup of coffee to building a company, there is a cooperative context: they *both agree* it is important to do it."

"Cooperation," I continued, "is when the parts give priority to the whole. An obvious example is the parts of our physical bodies. When healthy, our lungs, hearts, liver, knees, and nose are all cooperating for the health of our bodies. Disease, such as cancer, is when some of the cells stop cooperating.

"So if cooperation, not competition, is the fundamental process in nature everywhere, the universe is an indivisible whole, just as Lao Tzu, Confucius, Buddha, Moses, Jesus, Muhammad, Gandhi, Martin Luther King, Jr., Albert Einstein, and all the other greats concluded. No one has found the beginning, end, or edge of the universe. We do not understand how this can be, but there is much more we still also do not yet understand.

"What is important," I would continue, "is we recognize that cooperation is the fundamental process in nature and cannot be escaped. *Competition, compromise, consensus,* and *love* are four levels of maturity of cooperation. Cooperation is only the opposite of competition in the dualistic system called 'a human language'; there is no opposite of cooperation in nature. It is fundamental and inescapable.

"The universe is an indivisible whole and cooperation is when the parts give priority to the whole. This is how we each currently experience things occurring within our skins. When this is observed in our physical bodies we realize this is also how things relate with each other inside the universe. Reality is not a contradiction where cooperation is primary inside our skins but competition is primary everywhere else."

With the few interested in going this far into the conversation, frankly to my surprise, there was full agreement with what I was saying.

I now wish I had also said the following to each of them. This would have made it abundantly obvious that cooperation is fundamental and inescapable:

peting or cooperating with your lungs? It is self-evident that
sistent relationship of cooperation. Are the dirt, air, water, and
mpeting or cooperating to grow the plants that sustain us? It
they are primarily cooperating."

As we will see below, when we drop all of our current beliefs and take a
look at our immediate and direct experiences it is obvious that cooperation
is the fundamental process in nature and that maturation is the particular
kind of cooperation that is the fundamental process in nature. The air is in
a constant relationship of cooperation with our lungs and once we learn to
walk we stop crawling. And once we discover democracy we do not go back
to choosing dictatorship.

Soon, I suspect, there will be some enlightened corporate leaders who will
anticipate this maturation of our thinking into the higher layers of the skill of
self-consciousness. They will also become aware that, relative to one another,
cooperating with their competitors for the common good will not cost them a
penny: if appropriate they can equally increase their prices. And the company
that gives priority to the common good in all it does and increases prices the
least will have the competitive edge. This will also get their companies out in
front of this maturation of the public's thinking.

Then, while fully doing both, they will genuinely give priority to the common good and second priority to competition.

As mentioned earlier, they will reach direct common good agreements
with their competitors, such as raising their minimum wage to a livable wage,
donating the same percentage of profits to reduce poverty, and establishing environmental and safety standards beyond what governments are demanding.
They will welcome creditable third party common good as well as financial
audits so the public will respect and trust them to provide this leadership into
common good capitalism. Appropriate to the risk, they will eventually put a
cap on the annual return to equity investors, a high cap for startup companies
and a cap somewhere below 15% for duopolies. Any excess will be available
to provide this return during years that for whatever reason the company financially underperforms. This will make their stock very attractive to
investors investing for college expenses for their children and retirement.

Finally, executives will seek to have their incomes from the company be appropriate rather than to seek the highest income possible. This will also result in a shrinking of the difference in compensation between the highest and lowest paid employee.

As you will read below, each time we as societies have matured to the next layer in the skill of self-consciousness it has been experienced as a major shift because it always is a major shift. When growing up we each personally experience this. Giving priority to getting what we *want* as a child is very different from simply expressing our *feeling* of happy–not happy as a toddler. Giving priority as a teenager to our ability and right of *individual freedom* is very different from giving priority to getting what we want as a child. As an adult, giving priority to our freely chosen *fundamental belief* is very different from giving priority to our ability and right of individual freedom as a teenager.

It is the same for societies.

As a now global society we are ready to enter the next layer of maturity in the skill of self-consciousness. This is where we know in our direct experience that the universe is an indivisible whole. Therefore we naturally and effortlessly give priority to the common good, to the maturation of us all, and second priority to the self-interests of our physical bodies. It is why we love raising children. It is why we love participating in a constructive way in our community. It is why we enjoy love more than conflict. We also notice that this is a better set of priorities for the self-interest of our physical bodies: we experience a greater degree of cooperation with all those around us and we find that we have fewer enemies.

Maturation is the fundamental process in nature and it cannot be stopped. We are now ready to mature into self-consciously together structuring our societies so we, and all of our groups, are freely choosing to give priority to the common good, to moral behavior.

One of the purposes of this book is to assist you to understand that this next major maturation in the skill of self-consciousness is inevitable.

On its own it may be slow to occur. However when the public learns of the rapid expansion of duopolies in more product areas each day and begins to react negatively, cooperation for the common good by duopolies will begin to occur out of self-protection. This will result in the realization among us all that we can, indeed, give priority to cooperation, second priority to competition, and do both fully. We do it in sports all the time. As described in the editorial, a soccer league is a set of agreements that is the cooperative context. The entire season the competing teams give these agreements priority and competition between teams occurs as a second priority.

To the surprise of many, this more mature way of thinking will be pushed forward the most by corporate leaders seeking to sustain their duopoly positions by converting their companies into common good corporations.

It will become increasingly clear to all that the duopoly monopolies are already cooperating primarily by joining in each other's price increases. It will also be clear that we do not want to end the existence of these companies because they are doing a good job of efficiently providing us all that we need. It will then be discovered by all that the best step forward will be for the board members and executives of these duopolies to mature to where they freely choose to give priority to the common good. They will then also freely choose to reach cooperative agreements with each other.

In other words, the duopolization of the economy will make it much easier to mature to common good capitalism. Primarily only two (or three or four) companies will need to reach direct agreements to cooperate for the common good.

If not at first involved the other smaller competitors will then either join with them in these agreements or be called out by the press and on the Internet as not doing so, which will be very detrimental to their businesses.

Of course, the first idea of many will be to break up these companies to enhance competition. However, it would not be an easy task for governments to break up duopolies. They are usually global corporations. As mentioned already, they are also well organized and provide all the things we need. Aside from being logistically difficult to accomplish, it is not practically possible in today's world of easy access to just about any information. Whether two or ten dominant companies in a product, it is now easy to indirectly and primarily cooperate by matching each other's fundamental price increases. Thus maturation into respecting that cooperation is the inescapable fundamental process in nature is the only option.

Then, to the surprise of many on both the political left and right, the leaders of these companies will become some of the strongest advocates of the maturation of the thinking of us all into the higher layers of maturity in the human skill of self-consciousness we are now ready to master. They will know it is the only way their duopoly monopolies will be allowed to remain in existence. They will then be supported by the public at primarily and directly cooperating with their duopoly partners to reach agreements that give priority to the common good while fully continuing to compete as their second priority.

Then no one will want to go back to giving priority to competition in the marketplace. We will want it second in priority for its creativity and to sustain each person's right of free choice in a free market. It will also allow free markets to continue. Any new company can still enter a duopoly product market with a better idea and could potentially someday replace one of the two dominant companies in a product market.

The ease with which at Davos each of these economic leaders agreed with these ideas convinced me that we would soon mature capitalism into common good capitalism.

2

Duopolization

JOHN MACKEY IS THE FOUNDER AND CO-CEO OF WHOLE Foods, Inc. In November 2008, on the first day at his first Conscious Capitalism Conference, at lunch I sat down next to someone I didn't know. The first thing I asked him was what he did. He said, "I have just retired as head of marketing for P&G." P&G, I knew, is the largest consumer products company on Earth. Seizing the opportunity, I immediately asked him how many products they had. He said, "250." I then asked, "How many are number one or two in their market sector?" He immediately responded, "Every one of them." I later discovered that they used to have over 1,000 products and they are now down to only 250. If not easily able to create a duopoly, they have concluded that the wise thing to do is to get out of that product market. They are currently working their way down to 200 products.

In 1981 Jack Welch, then the CEO of General Electric, gave a speech at their annual meeting in which he stated that if your company is not number one or two in a product sector you should get out of it. What was he saying?

He was saying that a monopoly is illegal but a duopoly monopoly is legal.

As also described earlier, a duopoly monopoly is when two companies control a very high percentage of the market for a product.

If you had your choice of being one of many competitors in a product sector or one of two that together dominated that product sector, and your highest priority is the financial return to your shareholders, which would you choose, competition or a duopoly monopoly? You would be considered naïve to not take advantage of a duopoly monopoly opportunity if it presented itself or you could create it. At least since 1981 when Jack Welch publicly spoke these words, like P&G the highest priority in the corporate community has been to become number one or two in each product market or get out of it.

Many people are not aware of the duopolization that is happening in our USA and global economy. In this chapter I will provide some information on this so you can begin to watch for it.

Today the highest priority of all large corporations is to have products that are number one or two in their market so together the two companies control a large portion of the market. Then, without ever needing to talk to each other they can mutually control that product market, mainly by matching each other's fundamental price increases and buying any successful new entry into that market. There will still be competition between them at the secondary level of pricing, product design, packaging, and marketing. And anyone is free to come up with a better idea and go into business in competition with the duopolies so a free market is sustained. However the most important choice, price, *is easily and indirectly coordinated* by the duopolies to sustain a good profit by simply matching each other's fundamental price increases.

If any new and creative product does emerge in the territory of a duopoly monopoly and becomes popular, one of them will probably buy it. This recently happened in the world of Ben & Jerry's and Häagen Dazs.

Talenti became a new and popular super premium gelato. It began to eat into the sales of both of the duopoly companies. Nestlé, the owner of Häagen Dazs, and Unilever, the owner of Ben & Jerry's, the number two and three largest consumer products companies on Earth, ended up in a competition to buy it. Unilever won and now owns Talenti.

Initially the owners of Talenti did not want to sell. In Argentina one of the founders had discovered a wonderful gelato recipe and he dedicated himself to bringing it to the public. However, when they realized that their creative new kind of super premium gelato could be easily copied, when they also realized that it was already being copied by Häagen Dazs, and that the greater marketing and distribution efficiencies of the duopolies could end their continued successful emergence, they sold. This is the fate of most successful new products that come to market today. Their choice is to sell or be copied, experience price wars, and be easily outcompeted. So eventually they nearly always ultimately sell to one of the two large duopolies or triopolies.

If you live in the USA, next time you go to the supermarket, take a look in the ice cream freezers. You used to see about eight shelves of Ben & Jerry's and eight shelves of Häagen Dazs. You will notice that both now display less than eight shelves and Talenti has a significant number of shelves right next to them, only now both Talenti and Ben & Jerry's are owned by Unilever. You wouldn't know that from witnessing their brand names alongside each other in the freezer. Häagen Dazs now has its own gelatos as well and sometimes gets more shelf space as a result.

This is another strategy of the duopolies. They offer many brand name products, yet it is not obvious that the same company owns them. Next time you go into a convenience store, take a walk past the wall of refrigerator windows. See if you can guess how many of the brands of cold drinks are owned by Coca Cola or Pepsi.

Today all entrepreneurs know that, if it is not appropriate to do a public offering, they will someday sell their companies to one of the few largest companies in their market. The efficiency and breadth of their distribution systems usually necessitates this choice. The other option is not attractive: be skillfully copied and squeezed out of the market by the two dominant companies.

So look around where you live. As mentioned earlier, if you are in the USA you will notice that the two dominant pharmacies are CVS and Walgreens. The two dominant hardware and lumberyards are Home Depot and Lowe's. The two dominant package delivery companies are FedEx and UPS. The two dominant credit card companies are Visa and MasterCard. The one dominant search engine is Google. Facebook has a virtual monopoly in its market.

Let me provide additional examples so you will gain an awareness of just how extensive the near duopolization of the economy has become.

Six media giants now control 80% of what we read, watch, and listen to. In 1983 there were fifty media companies in the USA; there are now only the big six: GE, NewsCorp, Disney, Viacom, Time Warner, and CBS (a sixopoly monopoly). Four airlines—Delta, United, Southwest, and American— now control 80% of airline seats in the USA (a quadropoly monopoly). As measured by the number of seats available, at 40 of the largest 100 airports, a single airline controls a majority of the market. This is up from 34 airports ten years ago. One or two airlines control a majority of the seats at 93 of the top 100 airports.

MasterCard and Visa control 80% of the world's credit cards. Nike and

Adidas control 70% of soccer shoe sales globally. Verizon and AT&T control 84% of cellular service. Three companies make jet engines: Boeing, GE, and Siemens. A triopoly dominates auto rentals: Hertz, Avis, and Enterprise. And in 1995 the six largest bank holding companies had assets equal to 17% of US GDP. At the end of 2006 it was 55%. In 2010 it was 64%. It is now 70%. They are J.P. Morgan-Chase, Bank of America, Citigroup, Wells Fargo, Morgan Stanley, and Goldman Sachs.

Dollar Tree and Dollar General now control their market. Ninety percent of Clorox's brands are number one or two in their product sector. Ninety percent of Red Hat's products are number one or two in their sectors. Altera and Xilinx dominate program logical devices. We are down to four dominant health insurance companies: Aetna just bought Humana, Anthem is buying Cigna, UnitedHealth Group, and Blue Cross Blue Shield. In 24 of the 42 states the two largest health insurers control 70% or more of the market.

There are three dominant rating agencies for securities: Moody's, McGraw Hill–S&P and Fitch. Now there are only two companies that make one of our most important products to support human life: insulin; they are Eli Lilly and Novartis. Four corporations, led by Walmart, control more than half of grocery sales—Walmart gets more than one quarter of every grocery dollar spent in the US. Three companies, Monsanto, DuPont, and Syngenta, own 47% of the world's seeds; they own 65% of the global proprietary maize market. Just four corporations control nearly every major commodity, such as wheat, corn, and soy. Just four corporations control more than 80% of our meat supply. Two companies dominate the mining equipment market: Joy Global and Caterpillar. Boeing and Airbus supply over 82% of passenger aircraft in the world. Google's Android and Apple's iOS make up 96.3% of smartphone operating systems.

Many are aware of the big four accounting firms: Deloitte Touche Tohmatsu, Ernst & Young, Pricewaterhouse Coopers, and KPMG. How about the following dominant players in fast foods: McDonalds, Burger King, Subway, and Yum! Brands (Taco Bell, KFC, Pizza Hut, WingStreet, Long John Silver's, and A&W Restaurants)? Mars and Hershey control over 70% of candy production. Coca Cola and Pepsi control nearly 70% of syrup and flavoring production. Coca Cola, Pepsi, and Dr. Pepper Snapple Group

A LIST OF THE COMPANIES THAT CONTROL 80% OR MORE OF A PRODUCT MARKET IN THE USA AS OF JUNE 2016

Amusement Parks	%
The Walt Disney Company	52.4
NBC Universal Media LLC	22.1
SeaWorld Parks & Entertainment	8.3
Cedar Fair LP	8.1
Six Flags Inc.	7.5
TOTAL	98.4

Automobile Engine & Parts Manufacturing	%
Fiat Chrysler Automobiles	17.9
Toyota Motor Corporation	17.7
General Motors	14.5
Honda Motor Co. Ltd.	12.1
Ford Motor Company	10.2
Hyundai-Kia Automotive Group	9.0
Nissan Motor Co. Ltd.	8.7
TOTAL	90.1

Battery Manufacturing	%
Johnson Controls Inc.	24.6
Duracell	23.0
East Penn Manufacturing Co. Inc.	14.5
EnerSys Inc.	10.1
Exide Technologies	9.2
Energizer Holdings Inc.	6.4
TOTAL	87.8

Cable Providers	%
Comcast Corporation	40.3
Time Warner Cable Inc.	20.6
Cox Enterprises Inc.	9.6
Charter Communications Inc.	8.4
Cablevision Systems Corporation	5.2
TOTAL	84.1

Candy Production	%
Mars Inc.	34.5
The Hershey Company	22.7
Ferrara Candy Company	13.4
Mondelez International	9.5
TOTAL	80.1

Cereal Production	%
General Mills Inc.	28.0
Kellogg Company	27.3
Post Holdings Inc.	20.9
PepsiCo Inc.	6.1
TOTAL	82.3

Chocolate Production	%
The Hershey Company	29.6
Mars Inc.	21.8
Nestlé SA	11.6
Mondelez International	10.1
Lindt & Sprungli	7.3
TOTAL	80.4

Cigarette & Tobacco Manufacturing	%
Altria Group Inc.	57.5
Reynolds American Inc.	28.4
TOTAL	85.9

Credit Bureaus & Rating Agencies	%
Experian PLC	26.1
Equifax Inc.	19.9
McGraw Hill Financial Inc.	17.5
Moody's Corporation	16.1
Trans Union LLC	11.2
TOTAL	90.8

Custody, Asset & Securities Services	%
State Street Corporation	33.4
JPMorgan Chase & Co.	22.8
The Bank of NY Mellon Corp.	17.6
Citigroup Inc.	8.6
TOTAL	82.4

Department Stores	%
Target Corporation	37.4
Sears Holdings Corporation	13.2
Macy's, Inc	12.6
Walmart Stores Inc.	10.1
JCPenney Company, Inc	7.8
Nordstrom, Inc.	7.3
TOTAL	88.4

Explosives Manufacturing	%
Incitec Pivot Limited	44.6
Orica Limited	44.3
TOTAL	88.9

Fabric, Craft & Sewing Supplies Stores	%
Michaels Stores Inc.	47.7
Jo-Ann Stores Inc.	26.5
Hobby Lobby Stores Inc.	19.1
Hancock Fabrics Inc.	6.0
TOTAL	99.3

Greeting Cards & Other Publishing	%
Hallmark Cards Inc.	61.9
American Greetings Corporation	22.9
Visant Holding Corporation	10.5
TOTAL	95.3

Gypsum Product Manufacturing	%
USG Corporation	29.6
New NGC Inc.	20.0
Georgia-Pacific LLC	14.6
Eagle Materials Inc.	8.7
CertainTeed Corporation	7.7
TOTAL	80.6

Home Improvement Stores	%
Home Depot Inc.	48.4
Lowe's Companies Inc.	34.6
Menard Inc.	5.6
TOTAL	88.6

Internet Publishing & Broadcasting	%
Alphabet Inc.	27.2
Apple Inc.	22.4
Facebook	20.1
Netflix Inc.	10.7
TOTAL	80.4

Iron Ore Mining	%
Cliffs Natural Resources Inc.	41.6
United States Steel Corp.	32.6
ArcelorMittal	9
TOTAL	83.2

Major Household Appliance Manufacturing	%
Whirlpool Corp.	37.8
AB Electrolux	20.6
General Electric	13.0
AO Smith	5.4
LG Electronics	5.1
TOTAL	81.9

Oxygen & Hydrogen Gas Manufacturing	%
Praxair Inc.	36.3
Air Products & Chemicals Inc.	26.5
The Linde Group	18.3
Air Liquide	7.8
TOTAL	88.9

Petroleum Refining	%
Valero Energy Corporation	14.4
Exxon Mobil Corp.	14.2
Marathon Petroleum Corp.	13.1
Phillips 66 Company	12.1
Royal Dutch Shell PLC	10.9
Chevron Corp.	10.1
Tesoro Corporation	5.6
TOTAL	80.4

Rail Transportation	%
B'ton Northern Santa Fe Corp.	30.1
Union Pacific Corporation	29.6
CSX Corporation	14.4
Norfolk Southern Corporation	13.3
TOTAL	87.4

Refined Petroleum Pipeline Transportation	%
Kinder Morgan	30.2
Magellan Midstream Prtnrs L.P.	21.0
Enterprise Products Prtnrs L.P.	20.8
Buckeye Partners, L.P.	12.4
TOTAL	84.4

Satellite TV Providers	%
DirecTV Inc.	53.3
Dish Network LLC	29.4
TOTAL	82.7

Search Engines	%
Alphabet Inc.	78.2
Yahoo! Inc.	9.2
Microsoft Corporation	7.2
TOTAL	94.6

Space Vehicle & Missile Manufacturing	%
Lockheed Martin Corporation	32.0
Raytheon Company	23.9
The Boeing Company	11.3
Orbital ATK Inc.	7.6
Aerojet Rocketdyne Holdings	6.3
TOTAL	81.1

Truck & Bus Manufacturing	%
Daimler AG	36.0
PACCAR Inc.	20.3
AB Volvo	17.9
Navistar International Corp.	15.1
TOTAL	89.3

Warehouse Clubs & Supercenters	%
Walmart Stores Inc.	69.4
Costco Wholesale Corp.	18.0
TOTAL	87.4

Wireless Telecom Carriers	%
Verizon Wireless	37.9
AT&T Inc.	32.7
Deutsche Telekom AG	14.1
Sprint Nextel Corporation	12.9
TOTAL	97.6

control 64% of soft drink production. If Anheuser Busch-InBev succeeds in purchasing MillerCoors it will control 70% of beer production. Altria Group and Reynolds Lorillard control 85% of cigarette and tobacco production. Berkshire Hathaway, Mohawk Industries, and Interface control 62% of carpet and rug mills. And Gruma S.A.B. de C.V. and Grupo Bimbo S.A.B. control 74% of the tortilla production.

Ten companies—Coca-Cola, PepsiCo, Unilever, Danone, Mars, Mondelez International, Kellogg's, General Mills, Nestlé, and Associated British Foods—are the world's most powerful food and beverage companies; they control nearly everything we buy in those center aisles at the grocery store. 56% of ice cream production is controlled by Unilever (25%), Nestlé (18%), and Dean Foods (13%). 68.2% of snack foods are controlled by Frito Lay (51%), Con Agra (6%), General Mills (5.7%), and Kraft Foods (5.5%). 60.8% of coffee production is controlled by Sara Lee (24.3%), Kraft (14.1%), Nestlé (12.2%), and J. M. Smucker (10.2%). 87.9% of tea production is controlled by Pepsi (35.1%), Ferolito, Vultaggio & Sons (31.2%), Dr. Pepper Snapple Group (13.1%), and Coca Cola (8.5%). 57.9% of wine production is controlled by E & J Gallo Winery (25.5%), Constellation Brands (19,2%), and The Wine Group (13.2%). 79.5% of liquor and spirit production is controlled by Diagio (28.3%), Pernod Ricard (19%), Brown Forman (17.7), and Fortune Brands (14.5%). 68% of prefabricated home manufacturing is controlled by Berkshire Hathaway (48%), Palm Harbor Homes (7%), Champion Enterprises (7%), and Fleetwood Enterprises (6%). And Potash and Mosaic have a duopoly monopoly in fertilizer. Our most essential human resource is food, and fertilizer is necessary to grow most foods.

(Some of this information was found in *Market Domination! The Impact of Industry Consolidation on Competition, Innovation, and Consumer Choice* by *Stephen G. Hannaford, Praeger Publishers, Westport, CT, 2007. The rest can be found at the US Government Census Bureau website: https://www. census.gov/econ/concentration.html).*

More companies are also beginning to use surge pricing, now possible by technological advances in data gathering and analysis. A business identifies when another sells out of a product and automatically bumps up its price on it. This is another example of how the Information Age is changing the marketplace. Airlines have been doing this for a long time but it is now being done by others as well.

Today much of the merger and acquisition activity on Wall Street is for the purpose of companies becoming duopoly monopolies. They do not need to talk to each other to operate effectively as duopolies. They all went to the same kind of business schools and our communication systems now allow them to know just about everything the other company is doing. Although at their business associations the main players do actually often talk to each other, they do not need to directly talk with each other about the activities of their businesses, such as pricing and new designs for their products. They can quickly witness it in the market and respond. So lawyers are usually present at all board and management meetings to be sure they do not accidentally do anything, or put something in their minutes, that could be seen as "direct collusion for self-interest," which is illegal.

Yet today the priority of duopolies is "legal indirect collusion" both to sustain their duopoly monopoly position and to jointly have pricing power.

At a Ben & Jerry's board meeting a few years ago our CEO reported that, since Häagen Dazs had many two-for-one sales the previous year, our share of the super premium ice cream brand market in the USA that year went down from 44.2% to 44.1% and theirs went up from 42.2% to 42.3%. However this year we had more two-for-one sales than they did and we are back up to a 44.2% market share.

To have a little fun I said, "Well, why don't we talk to Häagen Dazs and agree to not have those two-for-one sales anymore. We and our customers would all be better off!"

Well, as you can imagine, the Unilever lawyer in the room spilt his coffee all over his papers as he abruptly jumped forward, shouting, "Don't put that in the minutes!"

"Just kidding! Just kidding!" I exclaimed as if I was startled that they didn't know I was just having a little fun.

I was having a little fun, something we easily do at Ben & Jerry's board meetings. However I was also making a point. I was humorously pointing out that it would be beneficial for both of our businesses and the custom- ers (a lower regular price because of lower costs) if we did reach such an agreement, but it is obvious that we cannot directly do that legally. So we play these competitive games as a secondary activity of competition for increased market share when we are really *primarily and indirectly cooperating* and need to be sure we never openly admit it. And the lawyer is in the room to make sure we never do. That is why he jumped into action so suddenly and passionately that he spilt his coffee. He needed to make sure we continue to behave as if competition is what we are primarily doing, even though it was obvious to at least some of us in the room that that is not true. What is always most important is not what we are secondarily doing but what we are primarily doing.

In the corporate community today, as much as possible competition is to be avoided. Cooperation is the fundamental process in nature and is now the self-conscious fundamental process in the corporate community. They are fully aware that if they do not participate in this maturation of the marketplace, two other companies will, and they will be left out. Therefore, as they accurately see it, they do not have a choice but to participate in building duopoly monopolies.

Stop and think about it. If our primary goal is to make money for our shareholders, wouldn't it be wise to get rid of all our products that are not one or two so we would have a duopoly position with all of our remaining products? We could then focus on maintaining mutual control of those product areas. We could also focus on expanding their sales territories so we were an immovable global company and could virtually guarantee a good, steady profit.

For instance, Nestlé and Unilever know that Häagen Dazs and Ben & Jerry's are the two dominant super premium ice cream brands in the USA. They have each expanded these brands into almost the same thirty-five nations around the globe. They know that they will eventually be the two dominant super premium brands on Earth. It is simply a matter of time.

This "silent duopoly cooperation" is the multinational ethic of the day because the leaders in corporations do not see themselves as *primarily members of societies* where they and their organizations agree to give priority to the common good. As we will see in *Chapter 4 – Layers of Maturity of the Skill of Self-consciousness,* they are still operating as if one of the middle layers of the skill of self-consciousness is the highest layer.

Since most of us are still operating on it as well, it is not easy for any of us to discover and embrace the next layer.

It is all of us, the entire human species, who are ready and able to mature to the next layers in the skill of self-consciousness. Once we mature into the next higher layers from where most of us are now, as is always the way with maturation, it will change everything in a good way.

We will understand that cooperation is the fundamental process in nature and maturation is the particular kind of cooperation that is fundamental. As in sports, we will continue competition because it is fun, stimulates creativity, and honors our ability and right of individual freedom.

However it will now always be secondary in importance.

As is the fundamental agreement in any human society, our priority will be *open and direct self-conscious cooperation* for the safety and maturation of us all. And all involved—owners, employees, customers, vendors, and suppliers—will primarily experience their work lives as meaningful, as a contribution to maturation on what we agree is the particular common good in our particular situation.

The responsibility of each generation is to have the next generation born into a more mature consensus of what is the common good. As the Elder and Mature Elder Layers of maturity become known by more and more people, like each of the lower layers, it is only a matter of time before they become common knowledge into which each child is born and raised to know and master as skills.

3
Movements

Ultimately this maturation into common good capitalism will primarily be the result of a common good movement.

Herein and throughout the rest of this book we will only be focused on describing a common good movement, not a political movement. As described in the editorial, a *political movement* is when people come together to move some policies into legislation. It includes electing candidates to help do it. A *common good movement* is people joining forces to mature something in the way we all think. Not just some of us but all of us.

If the universe is an indivisible whole then the natural highest priority of every part of it is to cooperate with the other parts for the good, the maturation, of the one whole. About this no part has a choice. This is part of nature.

If this is true, then at full maturity in the skill of self-consciousness the highest natural priority of all human beings is the common good. At this point it is also the natural highest priority of all societies of people. Yet in the world there are many actions perceived as evil. So obviously this is the result of people operating as if on of the lower layers of maturity in this skill is the highest layer, almost always without knowing they are doing it.

In 1979 I had the good fortune to travel throughout India and live for days with many of the people still alive who had worked closely with Mahatma Gandhi, the father of Indian independence and a promoter of nonviolent actions to bring about social maturation. Along the way I had also read his autobiography, many of his writings, and other books about him.

On my last train ride to Calcutta to take an airplane home, I sat on the steps of the train between two of the railroad cars just to get closer to what I was witnessing. The train bounced and screamed through the hot night. In the darkness I could see fires burning in villages. There was almost never a time in India when you could not see people and I wanted to fully drink in the beauty of the Indian life and culture I had come to love.

I then asked myself this question, "After all this reading and these conversations, what in my own words would I say is the main thing that Gandhi figured out?"

This is the answer that came into my thinking.

Gandhi figured out that at any one moment there are four things going on inside each human being:

Primary Intentions
Beliefs
Secondary Intentions
Behavior

Gandhi, in my judgment and because of his knowledge that the universe is an indivisible whole, came to the conclusion that every person's *primary intention* is good. About this none of us have choice. However our beliefs could be all over the map. Our *secondary intentions* and *behavior* flow from our beliefs.

It is people's beliefs that have them do evil things, not their primary intention.

This led me to conclude that the most important task is to assist people to embrace a more mature belief, what I have described as the Elder Layer of maturity in the skill of self-consciousness. Not just some people but all people.

Force should never be used and always fails because most people today value, as they should, their ability and right of individual free choice (Teen Layer). And each next layer builds on and in no way limits or negates the lower layers.

This is why Gandhi always announced in advance exactly his action of noncooperation with what he judged to be an immoral social law, such as India being a colony of England. This advance notice allowed all, *both in India and England*, to change their immoral behavior by reaching an agreement that ended the immoral social law, the legal crime. That would allow him to not take the planned action. He judged it his moral obligation to not cooperate with the immoral law. Therefore he had to act for the common good. But he did it in a way that gave priority to bringing about this change in as loving a way as possible. He focused on the belief in the established thought that made people comfortable sustaining the social tradition, a social tradition that was increasingly being seen as immoral due to the maturation of the thinking of the Indian and English people.

Years later this ultimately led me to ask the question, "What is the most loving way to bring about the maturation of a belief in a society?"

I realized there were four main groups in a society that had the most power to bring about maturation in our beliefs.

Not the most powerful in bringing about a change in a particular issue but a permanent maturation in a belief:

Politicians
Corporations
Consumers
Movements

At first I thought the politicians were the most powerful, the corporations second most powerful, consumers third most powerful, and movements the least powerful. But upon a deeper look at it I concluded it was the exact opposite.

The purpose of a movement is to mature something in the way we all think, not just in some of us but in all of us. That eventually changes consumer behavior. That eventually changes corporate behavior. And that eventually changes political behavior.

Secondly, a successful movement is usually a statement that a behavior that has been an acceptable social tradition is now accurately declared to be immoral, a legal crime. That is, as a society we have matured to where we now know it is not in alignment with our agreement to give priority to the common good. It is not something we can choose to do or not do. It is now declared to be a behavior we can no longer allow ourselves to do. As a society we have matured to where we now know it is immoral, not in alignment with our agreement to give priority to the common good.

The primary purpose of the Civil Rights Movement, the Women's Movement, the Environmental Movement, and the Gay Marriage Movement was to mature the way *we all think* about African-Americans, women, the environment, and gays. And the change sought was *mutual maturation in our thinking* necessary to continue to be in alignment with our agreement to give priority to the common good. The teachers of our children then begin to bring these *more mature ways of thinking* into the classrooms and when members of that generation become adults they assume it is normal to think in those more mature ways. This changes what they value as *consumers*.

Corporations need to make sure they are keeping the customers happy so they are quick to respond to this maturation of the thinking of all by, for instance, including African-Americans and people of all ethnic groups in their commercials.

Politicians are usually not able to pass legislation until it is supported by a majority of the public. Thus, the politicians, I realized, are usually the last to take action based on maturation in the way we all think. They may have the greatest power elsewhere, but they have the least power when it comes to bringing about a maturation in the thinking of us all.

This is how social maturation occurs in societies. It is primarily as a result of movements.

For instance the Environment Movement began in the 1960s. The Generation X and Millennial Generations have been brought up by grade school, high school and college teachers who loved developing in them a love and care for a sustainable environment. They now are in line in the USA to inherit $40 trillion. The result is that BlackRock, the largest asset manager in the US, just announced the launch of socially responsible mutual funds. And Morningstar, the primary evaluator of the performance of mutual funds, just announced they will not only provide a 5-star financial rating for mutual funds but also a similar rating, 5-globes, for the vast majority of funds, whether intended to be socially responsible or not. What started in the 1960s and 70s as an idea, socially responsible investing, is now becoming mainstream. Here, again, is a shout out of thanks to all the teachers reading this.

Now you know another reason I am writing this book. My hope is that you agree with the maturation in our thinking I am bringing to you so it stimulates the emergence of a movement toward a maturation of competitive capitalism into common good capitalism.

Lastly, many have argued that we should not use the word "capitalism" in the name of this movement. There is a reason the communist nations have moved into allowing capitalist economies. Fundamentally, capitalism is based on respect for individual freedom. It therefore is based on free markets for economic activity. This is an honoring of the Teen Layer of maturity in the skill of self-consciousness. So we need to build on it and not in any way negate it. The communist nations have come to the conclusion that they need to honor this layer of maturation in the skill of self-consciousness, at least in economic activity.

This honoring of the Teen Layer of maturity means that our maturation into common good capitalism needs to primarily be *a free choice in the private sector*. It cannot be successfully forced upon any individual or organization.

Ultimately it has to primarily be the result of a movement that matures something in the thinking of us all.

As mentioned a couple of times already and will be mentioned again, our democratic political systems were the result of the widespread maturation of the thinking of many into the Teen Layer of maturity in the skill of self-consciousness. There the priority is the honoring of our ability and right to exercise individual free choice. Today the governments of two-thirds of the nations on Earth are democracies. This maturation process has continued around the world and will naturally continue until all societies honor the Teen Layer of maturity in the skill of self-consciousness.

The next layer of maturity after the Teen Layer is the Adult Layer. This is where we give priority to our freely chosen fundamental belief. Although they differ widely, many of us are now operating at this layer of maturity in the skill of self-consciousness.

We are now ready to mature into the next higher layer after the Adult Layer. I have labeled it the "Elder Layer" and will thoroughly describe it in the next chapter.

So in my judgment the correct name for this movement is the "Common Good Capitalism Movement" or simply the "Common Good Movement." We need to build on individual freedom, not in any way negate it, by establishing common good capitalism as a possible free choice of individuals and organizations in the private sector.

Each person and organization needs to be free to choose it, reject it, or ignore it. It needs to primarily be the result of a common good movement and of each person studying his or her direct experience and concluding that common good capitalism is a more mature, and therefore more personally enjoyable, choice.

4
Mastering the Skill of Self-Consciousness

THERE ARE TWO THINGS THAT WILL BRING ABOUT THE maturation of capitalism into common good capitalism: individual maturation and a movement. In the last chapter I described how a successful common good movement is the most powerful force for change in a society because it results in a change in the way we all think. In this chapter I will go into detail in describing the seven layers of maturity of the skill of self-consciousness.

I firmly believe that many today are in transition from the middle layers of maturity in this skill into the higher layers. They will provide the leadership for this movement.

A Common Good Capitalism Movement will be one of the many expressions of their maturation into the higher layers of this skill. Thus it is essential that we understand these layers, how they build on one another, and that there is a highest layer that can be known by the time one is in one's late teenage years. In the next chapter, *Common Good Capitalism Movement,* I will describe the different ways individuals and organizations can play roles in this maturation of our economic lives together.

Allow me to begin this important chapter by telling some of the stories of my discovery of the middle and higher layers. I trust you will discover that some of them are similar to how you discovered some of these layers. Perhaps, like me, at first you did so without knowing you were discovering a layer of maturity in the skill of self-consciousness. You just thought you were discovering something new. After reading this chapter my hope is that you will in the future also have in your thinking a framework of layers of maturity and how anything new you learn fits into it. As you will discover, this is the practical way we integrate the third dimension of the skill of self-consciousness, the oneness of nature, into our thinking process.

When I was a sophomore in high school, during lunch period I received permission with two fellow players on the football team I greatly respected to go to our lockers to get our history books to study for a test. While walking down the empty hallway one of them said he had learned that milk causes pimples. We all had pimples. I said *"Really?"* in a way that, I can now see, was totally giving my power to them to such a high degree that the two of them fell all over themselves laughing at how easily I did it.

I grew up in the working class Austrian-Hungarian community in South Omaha, Nebraska, and was one of the first boys from our neighborhood to be accepted into Creighton Prep, the school far from our house that the wealthy Catholic boys in town attended. I definitely felt very inferior, especially to others on the football team who were the most respected boys in our school because in those years we were usually the state football champions.

When I closed my locker, which blocked my view of them, all I saw was their backsides as they rushed to the stairs to avoid going back to the lunchroom with me. It felt like to them I was a piece of scrap paper they had just wadded up and thrown in the wastebasket. I immediately sought an escape from returning to the lunchroom.

Across from our lockers was the chapel. I went in and sat down in the last pew. The chapel was empty of people, and there was no light except for the one red vigil light to the left of the altar. Very little light shone through the windows on the dark rainy day. So it was not easy to see the altar even though the chapel was small, a former classroom.

You need to know more about my upbringing to understand the following story. My father, Hienie, ran Mollner's Meat Market and his two brothers, Emerick and Leo, worked for him in the family business. Mollner's Meat Market was at the center of an Austrian–Hungarian community around Saint Joseph's Catholic Church and most of our community was from a peasant Austrian village, Apetlon. The older people still spoke their Austrian language instead of English. Like my four brothers I began working at the age of seven sweeping floors and cleaning the scales and counters at the end of the day.

While working in the backroom cleaning sausage-making machines, my Uncle Emerick periodically said to me, "Just remember kid, you are a peasant and you will always be a peasant." Each time I would quietly say to myself, "I am not! I am an American. I can be anything I want to be."

Although already matured by American society to know I was not stuck at being a peasant, I very much felt like a peasant at this wealthy students' high school.

Fighting deep sadness while sitting in the last pew, I eventually asked myself the question, "Who loves me?"

I thought of each person close to me in my life: my mother; father; sister; my two uncles who worked with my dad, my brothers, and me in Mollner's Meat Market; each of my brothers; my friends; my teachers; my coaches; the priests, the nuns, and others.

I couldn't honestly conclude that there was a single person who behaved lovingly toward me.

I also did not understand why the people around me did not relate in a more loving way with each other. It was obvious to me how good it would feel for all of us to be caring and kind toward each other.

"Why were those two guys unkind to me?"

"What is wrong with me?"

"Why are so many of my classmates unkind to each other?"

In deep sadness my head and lineman's shoulders eventually curled and I hunched over in the pew with my head hanging down very low. It felt like I was being chocked and tears began to fall on my pants.

Then my painful sadness suddenly turned to joy when, upon looking up and seeing the crucifix above the altar, I realized there was one person who loved me: "God loves me!"

I was suddenly ecstatic and sprung up into kneeling on the kneeler. There was one person I could honestly say loved me. The lines of tears on my cheeks began to crack as I smiled in the joy that there was one person who loved me. "God loves me!"

Then, just as quickly, my joy turned again to sadness and I slid back into sitting on the pew.

I realized that I already knew that God loved me. So why was I getting so excited about it? That hadn't made a difference in how I felt when those two guys abandoned me?

Then my attention turned to the fact that one moment I was extremely sad, the next moment I was extremely happy, and then the next moment I was sad again, all within less than a minute. Now I wanted to understand how those rapid changes in my experiences could so easily occur as a result of my thoughts. I did not know the answer to this question.

I pulled myself up onto the kneeler again. Through the rainy day darkness of the chapel I looked up at the altar and crucifix above it as if they were old friends but I knew they did not have the answer to this question. For a while I just watched the one red vigil light to the left of the altar flicker in the near darkness.

Then it became clear to me what I had to do.

I was going to take "a vow with myself to understand the meaning of life."

I did not understand how my experiences could change so easily. In fact I realized I did not understand much about life and I did not want to be ignorant anymore. I suddenly realized that there was one thing I knew for sure: I did not understand "the meaning of life." I did not understand why I should be doing one thing rather than another and I wanted to know the answer to this question.

Getting full of enthusiasm at this idea I stood up in the darkness and stepped into the aisle. I wasn't ready to leave the chapel, but I didn't want to be sitting or kneeling any longer. I was suddenly full of enthusiastic energy. I also didn't want to be following anyone's rules anymore. My body was shaking inside with excitement and it just had to move.

I looked around the chapel, enjoying my commitment to a mission that was far more important than those two guys liking me. Courage began to flow threw my veins and muscles and into my heart and brain. It was as if I had gone from being nearly dead to being fully alive again. I began to walk in no particular way around the aisle in the back of the chapel as if it were my bedroom and I was trying to think something through while talking out loud, something I sometimes did in my bedroom.

"This is important. I am going to do this," I said quietly a number of times. Disregarding the tradition to not speak in church I spoke it a little louder each time I said it with a greater sense of full commitment to it. If people were anywhere in the chapel they would have been able to hear me: "This is important. I am taking a vow with myself to discover the meaning of life!"

As I began to calm down I stopped moving about, stood still, and came up with a strategy.

To remain focused on this task I decided to attend the Mass at the beginning of the lunch period each day. I would use that time to think through things for the purpose of figuring out the meaning of life. Now nothing was going to be more important than this and this was one way I would remain focused on it.

I walked out of the chapel without genuflecting and back to the lunch room not at all concerned about what those two guys or anyone else thought of me. I had a reason for living that was far more important.

I did go to Mass every school day the rest of my high school years at Creighton Preparatory High School and all through my years at Creighton University as well. I had started a journal when I was younger and decided to be more committed to periodically writing in it to think things through there as well.

This in combination with making the sign of the cross each time I came out of the huddle—something the coach forced me to do because it was the way I remembered my right hand from my left hand so I would always get the plays right—got me chosen by the priests to be head of Sodality, the Catholic men's organization at the high school. I told them that making the sign of the cross was just so I would remember my right hand from the left, but they didn't believe me. That in combination with going to Mass every day got me chosen.

I became so focused on this priority that when the Jesuits told me that it could be my priority if I entered the priesthood, I entered it after my junior year of college. A year and a half into this commitment they told me I could not read a book I wanted to read, not a radical book but one written by another Jesuit, Pierre Teilhard de Chardin. It also became clear that this was just an example of a deeper problem that became obvious: I was primarily being trained to be a salesman of their beliefs. I came to the conclusion that they had broken their agreement to support me in my search for the meaning of life.

Even though my mother was devastated that I ended the tradition of having a child of a large Catholic family become a religious, I was not going to allow anything to limit my raw commitment to my goal. So I left the Jesuits.

Upon returning home I took long walks in circles on the grass in parks and concluded that I had given my power to the Catholic Church and that had been a mistake. I also realized that nearly everyone seemed to be primarily trying to sell me something like the priests who told me what I wanted to hear to get me to enter the seminary.

I concluded that I needed to keep my power and stop giving it away to any person or organization. Not to anyone or anything.

On a night a few weeks after returning from Saint Bonifacius Seminary I was walking and thinking things through on the circular path in the park behind the Administration Building at Creighton University. During that walk I decided to take what became my second of the three vows I have taken with myself during my life: I would solely go to my direct experiences to discover the meaning of life. Especially now that I felt betrayed by the institution that I thought would never betray me, I didn't feel I could trust anyone.

Before I left the park that night I concluded there were two beliefs that I already knew from my direct experiences to be true. First, there was always a reason for doing one thing rather than another. Second, I would only go to my direct experiences to discover truths because once I knew them there I was able to be certain I was correct: I could always look at my experiences again to be sure I was right. Like gravity, I could always do the equivalent of dropping a book on my foot to confirm my conclusion is accurate.

I didn't realize it at the time, but with this second vow I had made the switch from being *a believer* to being *a personal scientist*. The latter is some-one who *primarily studies his or her direct experiences* to identify the most fundamental belief all other chosen beliefs will honor.

I now believe becoming a personal scientist is essential for each of us to achieve full rather than partial freedom. It is also necessary to achieve full maturity in the skill of self-consciousness.

As described earlier, when we are living according to a belief, *any belief regardless of its content,* we are living our lives based on partial freedom in the belief it is full freedom. Since we are exercising free choice when we choose the belief, we think we are continuing to be in the experience of full freedom. However, from the point of choosing that belief onwards *our second priority is to obey it.* Our *priority* is no longer our ability and right of free choice. As will also be described later, in each moment it is always the priority that counts the most because it determines everything else.

To achieve full freedom and full maturity in the skill of self-consciousness we need to be a personal scientist. It is part of honoring the Teen Layer in exercising our responsibility of mastering the Adult Layer skill of giving priority to our fundamental belief.

For a personal scientist the choice of our most fundamental belief needs to be primarily the result of a study of our direct experience.

Since we can at any time again turn our attention to our direct experience to affirm it is true, we are not primarily obeying anything or anyone. Instead of giving our power to a second thing we keep it and therefore sustain our ability and right of true full freedom.

Sharing the importance of this is one of the main reasons I am writing this book. I am now aware that I and nearly all I know have spent most of our lives in partial freedom thinking it was full freedom as a result of giving our power to a bunch of words, called "a belief," rather than the knowledge we can in any moment affirm to be true in direct experience so it becomes a knowledge skill.

I then realized that to keep to these first two truths I had to do something else before I left the park: I had to throw out all the beliefs about life I had been brought up to think were true. If I did not do this, they would still be in play inside me, both self-consciously and unconsciously. Therefore, I had to make a commitment to abandon all of them or I would not be able to remain focused on primarily going to my direct experience to create a system of beliefs solely determined from a study of my direct experience. These beliefs would be *second in importance* and formed so I could talk with others and myself about them. The fact that I could affirm they were accurate by simply turning my attention to my immediate and direct experience would remain my priority and sustain the experience of full freedom. I would still have all of my power and be able to freely choose the best exact particular response in each situation without the presence of this second party, a belief I was *obeying*.

I was fully aware from my already keen interest in psychology that many of my beliefs were deep and unconsciously inside me. However I still needed to make this commitment. I knew I would eventually discover them active in my behavior and then be able to choose whether or not to keep them.

I became comfortable with these decisions, fully committed to this second vow, and ready to leave the park.

Then I realized that I had to make one more decision: "Is there a God? Am I also going to throw out that belief?"

I decided that I needed a couple more walks around the park to find the answer to this question and began to walk around it again. I came to the conclusion that if I held on to even one belief from the past I was not going to be able to *solely* go to my direct experience. Therefore, I had to also throw out this belief.

This felt like a very big decision. However, I was clear that I had to do it. I trusted that if God exists He, She, or It would also be discovered in the study of my direct experiences. So I let go of this most cherished of my beliefs as well. I wasn't going to let anything get in the way of me now going to my direct experiences to discover the meaning of life.

I left the park and returned to my dorm room in Deglman Hall. I felt fully comfortable with my first two chosen beliefs and my determination to primarily go to my direct experiences to discover any additional truths to guide my life.

Before I had left for the seminary I had been living at home and traveling to Creighton University each day. Upon returning from the seminary I had succeeded in being hired as a moderator of a floor at Deglman Hall. This was to also accomplish the goal of becoming free of my parents and the sociocultural limitations of our ethnic community.

As you will see below, without being aware of it, with my first vow I had graduated into the Adult Layer of maturity in the skill of self-consciousness. That is where we think things through and very self-consciously choose our most fundamental belief. As a sophomore in high school I had bungled into making a commitment to do that in response to the rejection by my two fellow football team members. Secondly and also without being aware of it, upon leaving the seminary I had bungled into graduating to the Elder Layer by deciding to give priority to discovering the most fundamental truth that all my other beliefs would honor by primarily going to my direct experiences to find my fundamental belief instead of choosing it from the many beliefs I would come upon. I had backed into doing both as a reaction to what I was experiencing. This, I have discovered and especially in the absence of eldering by wise elders, is the way most of us graduate up the layers of the skills of self-consciousness. We discover that it is only by discovering the next layer of maturity that we are able to reduce our thinking pain, the pain of not being able by choice to move more as one with all that is around us.

Everything is *conscious*. It is doing one thing rather than another. Dirt is being dirt, water is being water, air is being air, and the sun is being the sun. A chair is being a chair, an automobile is being an automobile, and a house is being a house. *Self-consciousness* is the ability to know what we are doing while we are doing it. It is being able to think about the past, plan for the future, and consistently execute the plan in the present. It also allows us to choose our self-definition. What I eventually discovered is that as we mature our self-definition matures.

When we become fully aware of the oneness of nature, we know we are first the universe that will not die and secondly our physical bodies that will die. It is this that results in our true self-interest becoming the common good of us all. And the consistent joy of happiness we each intuitively know is our birthright is the result of living according to this fully mature self-definition.

We are not born with the skill of self-consciousness. Like the learning of any skill, like riding a bicycle, each smaller skill builds on the one that came before it.

So we have to learn each smaller skill in the natural progression to master the full skill.

Just as there is a total skill of riding a bicycle there is a total skill of self-consciousness. We can always get better at executing both, but the basic skill has a certain number of smaller skills that build on one another, become habits, and result in the total habitual basic skill.

For instance, and as described earlier, when learning to ride a bicycle we have to first learn to hold it up so it does not fall down. We can't move on to focusing on mastering the second skill, putting our outside foot on the nearest pedal when it is near the ground and pushing off on it, until we have turned the skill of holding the bicycle up so it does not fall down into a habit.

Only then can we turn our full attention to learning the second skill without having to turn our attention back to holding the bike up so it does not fall down.

The same pattern exists when mastering each next smaller skill in the progression: ensuring the bike does not fall down when we glide on it, throwing our body up onto the seat, staying up while pedaling, and turning. Each time we have to turn the most recently learned smaller skill into a habit so we can turn our full attention to mastering the next skill without needing to turn our attention to the most recently learned smaller skill.

There are also smaller skills that build on one another and accumulate into the total human skill of self-consciousness. The difference between learning this skill and learning the skill of riding a bicycle is that we can learn to ride a bicycle in a day or two. Since the human brain is not fully developed until we are at least in our late teens, it is not easy to learn the total skill of self-consciousness until then.

What is important to note, especially for young people, is that we can master the full skill by the time we are entering our twenties.

What is second in importance to note is that in raising our children we want to give highest priority to their understanding from an early age that there are layers of maturity of the human skill of self-consciousness and there is a highest layer. They will then understand the importance of having us be part of their process of mastering the total skill. They will also know, hopefully by our example, that there is nothing more important for the achievement of the consistent joy of happiness than the mastery of the full human skill of self-consciousness.

There are many who do not grow up within families and communities that are aware of the existence of the layers of maturity of the skill of self-consciousness and of their importance. And there are many individuals and societies operating as if one of the lower layers is the highest layer. So let me now present what I understand to be the seven layers of the skill of self-consciousness. Hopefully this will stimulate much discussion by many of what are the layers. Just as we have reached widespread agreement that the Earth is round and it circles the sun, this will eventually lead to widespread agreement on a model.

There is a truth about the shape of the Earth, it can be represented in a human language, and we can all come to agree that representation is accurate. In the same way, there is a truth about the layers of maturation of the skill of self-consciousness; it can be represented in a human language; and we can come to agree that representation is accurate.

As I think you will come to agree, at the bottom our maturation from competitive capitalism into common good capitalism will be the result of our maturation in the skill of self-consciousness from what I will label in this chapter the "Adult Layer" and into the "Elder Layer" and "Mature Elder Layer." These are the layers where we become free of both inside and outside oppression. These are the layers where we discover we have been living in partial freedom and thinking it is full freedom. The Mature Elder Layer is the layer where we discover and fully and self-consciously embrace the *skill* of full freedom. Therefore it is essential that I take the time in this book to assist you to become aware of the layers of maturity of the skill of self-consciousness and how they naturally and effortlessly build on one another.

Economically our maturation into the Elder and Mature Elder Layers will be as significant a change in our lives together as, governmentally, our maturation from all forms of dictatorship into democracies.

Therefore becoming fully aware of the layers of maturity of the skill of self-consciousness and how they naturally and effortlessly build on one another is essential.

Throughout the ages there have been many models of the skill of self-consciousness. Some of them only included the lower layers because the originators did not know of the higher layers. Presented here is the model I have created from a study of my direct experiences.

You will, therefore, not witness me pointing to authorities or scientific studies to support what I write.

To escape voluntary inside oppression at the Mature Elder Layer we keep our power, all of it, rather than giving it to any other person or belief. At the Elder Layer that precedes it, we primarily study our immediate experience to identify our most fundamental belief. As I think you will come to agree, it is only a result of being a personal scientist, turning our attention to our immediate and direct experience, that we can learn and master these two knowledge skills as skills.

After reading this chapter and a study of your direct experiences, you may identify a different model from the one presented here. As you will see, that will be encouraged. At the Elder Layer each of us will create our model of the layers of maturity of the skill of self-consciousness. However to continue this presentation we will have to use my model. Hopefully both of our models will be similar and accurate.

There are seven layers in my model and below are the names for them, with the earliest layer at the bottom and the most mature layer at the top. There is also a chart representing them and our highest priority at each layer. I will then briefly describe each in the order in which we learn them.

A more thorough description of each can be found in other articles and books I have written. However it is essential that we become aware of them because it is this awareness that will lead to the natural maturation of capitalism business into common good business:

Mature Elder
Elder
Adult
Teen
Child
Toddler
Baby

THE SEVEN LAYERS OF MATURITY OF THE SKILL OF SELF-CONSCIOUSNESS	
PRIORITY	
Mature Elder	Self-Conscious Experience of the Oneness of Nature: Eldering
Elder	Accurate Fundamental Belief Using Personal Science That the Universe Is an Indivisible Whole
Adult	Fundamental Belief
Teen	Free Choice
Child	Wants and Relative Feelings
Toddler	Fundamental Feeling (happy-not happy)
Baby	Sensations

BABY

As a baby we are in an *unconscious state of experiencing ourselves as one with all things.* Our natural unconscious priority is to use our sensations to mature. Therefore, we have only one focus, to experience ourselves as sensually happy. This occurs when we are supported in maturing: all that is needed to accomplish this is for us to be kept safe and provided opportunities to mature. For instance, we feel safe when we receive enough milk, when nothing causes us pain or fear, or when we play with toys that enable us to master some sensual skills.

We do not yet know a human language, which would allow us to break the universe up into parts. We do not yet identify ourselves with some parts of the universe and not others, such as "I am an American." Therefore, our unconscious (non-self-conscious) experience is that we are all that exists.

Today the one place in public we comfortably look someone in the eyes and act as if we are that person as much as ourselves is when looking a baby in the eyes. A baby is in an unconscious experience of being one with all that exists and we know the baby will be happiest if we join him or her there. (Being totally receptive and behaving as if there is nothing primarily to fear is the self-conscious experience of the oneness of nature. We intuitively know it is safe to relate that way with a baby.)

Imagine what our lives were like when in the early days of human life we had our large brain, but we had not yet created a human language. We were in what Jon Young, the Father of the Art of Mentoring, calls "deep nature connection." We moved sensually at one with nature to survive. We could smell our way to water. We learned the language of the birds to find the wild dogs to get meat to eat. We had no experience of separation from nature. Jon assists people to discover the oneness of nature by providing opportunities for them to be in a deeply intimate relationship with it, the way babies are in a deeply intimate relationship with it.

TODDLER

Our mastery of the first of the three dimensions of the skill of self-consciousness begins to occur when we become *aware of difference*. The first one we become aware of is the *fundamental feeling* of happy–not happy. We will call this the "Toddler Layer."

At the Toddler Layer we are only aware of the most fundamental feeling of happy–not happy, the most fundamental feeling polarity represented in a language. This fundamental feeling is the feeling of happy (oneness) or not happy (not moving as one with all around us). It is only later that we break "not happy" into many positive and negative *relative feelings* such as mad, glad, sad, and scared.

As a toddler our priority is to have our *fundamental feeling* be happy rather than unhappy. It is the main *difference* we know.

As we will see later, all *relative feelings* have degrees of feeling them. On the scale of one to ten we could feel sad at a level 8 that our dog died. On the other hand, the *fundamental feeling of happy–not happy* is the only feeling that does not have degrees of feeling it: there are no degrees of oneness. We are either experiencing the fundamental feeling of happy (moving as one with all around us) or not feeling it. Therefore, we can't get better or worse at feeling the fundamental feeling of happy but there are degrees of the fundamental feeling of unhappy (relative feelings).

Also we can only be experiencing the feeling of fundamentally happy *as the container* within which everything else is occurring: our sensations, relative feelings, and beliefs. Or we are not feeling it as the container.

This, the recognition experientially of the most fundamental difference of happy–not happy, is the first dimension of the three dimensions of the skill of self-consciousness. The three dimensions are the following:

THE THREE DIMENSIONS OF
THE HUMAN SKILL OF SELF-CONSCIOUSNESS

1. The recognition of differences.
2. The creation of the mutually agreed upon human illusion tool of separate parts (time and space) that allows us to create our human languages and, in turn, become self-conscious.
3. The self-conscious experience of the oneness of nature.

As you will see, full mastery of the skill of self-consciousness is when we know all three and, while fully and simultaneously experiencing all three, self-consciously give priority to the experience of the oneness of nature, second priority to the use of the mutually created illusion tool of separate parts (human languages) to be self conscious, and third priority to differences (particularly the fundamental feeling of happy–not happy) as the container of whatever is occurring in our perception of separate parts.

Only at the Child Layer do we learn to be aware of relative feelings, such as mad, glad, sad, and scared, as distinct from the fundamental feeling of happy–not happy that does not have relative degrees of feeling it.

From the Toddler Layer on we either are or are not experiencing happiness as the container within which relative feelings occur as second in importance.

Relative feelings are the feelings we experience between our physical body and other people or parts of the universe. For a toddler the *fundamental feeling* of happy-not happy is the experience of our physical body in relationship with the entire rest of the universe. There are no degrees of this *non-self-conscious happy–not happy feeling* in the experience of a toddler. He or she is either fundamentally happy—moving happily as one with the universe—or to differing degrees not moving happily as one with the universe (unhappy).

CHILD

Next we learn a human language, what we will label the "Child Layer."

Without being aware of it, we all naturally begin behaving as if the fundamental assumption in language, *that the universe is an immense number of separate parts labeled with "words,"* is the accurate fundamental assumption about reality. It is not. This assumption is a *mutually created illusion tool* that allows us to create our elaborate human languages that, in turn, allows us to become self-conscious.

So the *mutually created human illusion tool* that there are separate parts is a valuable tool.

But it does not represent reality.

The assumption that there are separate parts represents the opposite of reality. It represents an illusion, but a very valuable illusion. It allows us to create our human languages that, in turn, allow the indivisible universe to mature to where it is able through us to be self-conscious at many locations at the same time.

Imagine two human beings sitting on the shaded jungle floor relaxing after having just eaten a full meal. It is a very long time ago, before we had created our human languages.

While playing around with a coconut, the first human being begins saying "wako wako" while playing with the coconut. The second human being realizes that the first human being is doing something she has never witnessed before. He is attaching a particular sound to the coconut. She goes over and puts her hand on his hand that is on the coconut and looks him in the eyes. She repeats the sound to him that he has been attaching to the coconut. She says "wako wako" while looking at him directly in the eyes. There are three other coconuts nearby. She then takes his hand and puts her hand on his on each of the other three coconuts. Each time she looks him directly in the eyes and says, "wako wako."

Here is a question for you. Without a human language what is the only way they could reach agreement to have the sound "wako wako" be the sound (the word) they will use to represent a coconut? You might want to have the fun of looking up from your reading to see if you can guess the answer before reading further. How do you think they were able to reach agreement without the existence of a human language? Take a few moments to come up with your best guess. Then read the next paragraph.

There is only one way they could have reached *agreement* without the existence of a human language: *they looked each other in the eyes and mutually experienced the fundamental feeling of happy rather than unhappy (the direct experience together of the oneness of nature—happiness—rather than conflict—unhappiness).*

Oneness is all things moving as one thing. When two people have this *mutual fundamental experience of happiness* it is what we have labeled "agreement." This is true even if it is only between the two of us and that is where our attention is focused. This is the relative experience of the oneness of nature, called "local oneness" or "agreement."

It is the direct self-conscious experience of the two of us moving as one thing. It is the local experience of the fundamental feeling of happiness. We are either in the experience of agreement (the fundamental feeling of happiness) or not in it (the fundamental feeling of conflict, unhappiness).

When we reach an agreement with another, where is the agreement? Can you point to it? Is it on the table, under the chair, in the backyard? Agreement does not have a location.

Agreement is a mutual and local self-conscious experience of oneness. Self-consciously it is only between the two of us. It is the feeling of peace (oneness) rather than conflict (separate pasts and competition). Still today we affirm agreement by looking each other in the eyes and acknowledging together the experience of peace (local oneness), the absence of the experience of conflict as the experiential affirmation of agreement.

You and I could reach an agreement to go to a movie tonight. That would be a relative moving as one: relative to one another the two of us are agreeing to move as one tonight. Or we could reach agreement, as those two human beings did while having their hands on the coconuts, to have the sound "wako wako" be the sound, the word, they will use to represent a coconut, thereby creating the first word of a human language.

Note that it is not possible to be partially in agreement. We are either in agreement or we are not in agreement. Agreement is the local experience of oneness. It is also the local experience of the fundamental feeling of happiness, the only feeling we are either fully feeling or fully not feeling.

When we reach full maturity in the skill of self-consciousness, we know how to always give priority to the fundamental feeling of happiness in relationship with the entire rest of the universe, not just locally. It becomes the natural and effortless container within which we always experience everything else.

At that point we are able to do this *no matter what else is occurring where we are standing.* Herein this is labeled as it has most often been labeled throughout history, the *fundamental feeling of "happy" rather than "not happy."* The *experience* of it has also often been labeled "enlightenment" in the East and "the state of grace" in the West. It is the skill of giving priority in our thinking to the direct experience of "deep nature connection." It is giving priority to *the experience of indivisible oneness of the universe as who we each primarily are* with our physical body parts of it being second in importance. Our actions while giving the experience priority is what we label "moral behavior": in action freely choosing to give priority to the common good because it sustains *the experience of happiness* as the container of all else we experience.

So the only way those two human beings looking each other in the eyes with their hands on the coconut could have, without already having created a human language, agreed on "wako wako" as the sound they would use to represent a coconut is by *mutually recognizing* they were having the *mutual experience* of moving as one. They became aware they were both experiencing the fundamental feeling of happy rather than unhappy. They would have recognized that *experience* as having reached what we now label in our languages "an agreement (moving as one)." In this case it was a *relative experience of oneness* on agreement to use "wako wako" to represent a coconut, the experience of only the two of them moving as one (local oneness).

However, without the universe being an indivisible whole, that is, without oneness being a fact, *the local experience of oneness, of agreement where their attention was focused, would not have been able to be experienced.* And without the *fundamental feeling experience of the oneness of nature always experienced as fully happy* rather than to some degree not happy, the agreement could not have occurred.

At the Child Layer of the learning of the skill of self-consciousness we are not aware of this. Therefore in the process of learning a human language we unconsciously assume the fundamental structure of the universe is the same as the fundamental structure of a language: like the words in a language it is an immense number of separate parts and we are each only one of them. Thus, our priority becomes our *wants.*

We unconsciously are defining ourselves as only our physical bodies—the only part of the universe over which we have sole and complete inside control.

Therefore, our new priority becomes getting what our physical bodies want.

We are now aware of having relative sensations and feelings such as milk-no milk, or money-no money. Our *priority* is getting what we *want* as if we are only our physical body and what we want is separate from it. So, if we can only have some of the dark chocolate covered cherries that are in a box on the kitchen table once we have kissed Uncle Charlie who stinks of cigar smoke that we hate, we run over and quickly kiss him and then run to the kitchen table to get some dark chocolate covered cherries. Now what our physical bodies want is more important than our *feelings* of disgust and the *smell* of cigar smoke we hate.

As we have all witnessed, children easily behave as want machines. They easily give *priority* to what they want. It is this priority each moment that defines the Child Layer.

TEEN

The next layer is the "Teen Layer." This is where we discover our ability and right to exercise individual freedom of choice. Up until now we have only been exercising free choice within the multiple-choice questions provided by others.

Now we realized that we could make up the multiple-choice questions.

For instance, before when mom asked us if we wanted chocolate, vanilla, or strawberry ice cream we would say "Chocolate." Now we may say, "I do not want to talk about ice cream right now. I want to talk about getting a car."

Now our *priority* becomes exercising our ability and right of *individual free choice* without unconsciously accepting an outside limitation, such as a multiple-choice question created by others.

Teens often become so excited about the discovery of direct and unrestrained freedom of choice that they begin wearing very different clothes and make very different choices from others to celebrate this newfound layer of maturity in the skill of self-consciousness.

ADULT

The next layer is the "Adult Layer." This is where we discover that our most important free choice is our *fundamental belief.* When we self-consciously choose our most fundamental belief, all of our other beliefs and behavior choices yield to it. In our thinking our lives are now experienced as meaningful: there is always a known reason for doing one thing rather than another.

We unconsciously give our power to our freely chosen fundamental belief, *and therefore our second priority is to obey it.* This is the result of also unconsciously sustaining in our thinking the fundamental pattern of behavior we have been using to survive since birth, the giving of our power to another, usually our parents.

However, now in our thinking we are giving our power to an internally and voluntarily created and chosen parent: a belief.

Outside and Inside Oppression

As mentioned earlier, full freedom is only achieved when a person becomes free of both inside and outside oppression. *Outside oppression* is when another is dominating us. *Voluntary inside oppression* is when one gives priority to another person or a belief.

It doesn't make any difference what is the content of the belief.

From the moment a belief is given priority, one's second priority is to *obey* that belief. Our ability to exercise free choice has ended. Yet we believe we are continuing to exercise free choice because we freely chose the belief.

As will be fully described below, the only way to be fully free of this voluntary inside oppression is to keep one's power, all of it, and use it to primarily study one's immediate direct experience to identify the accurate fundamental truth that will guide one's life.

The result will be full freedom: one can at any time turn one's attention to direct experience and witness that it is accurate.

One has also sustained the ability to exercise free choice in the future. One still has all of one's power and there is not a second thing, a belief, which has to be given the power of leading us before we can act.

However, none of this is understood at the Adult Layer. The priority at this layer is one's freely chosen fundamental belief and obeying it.

Usually our freely chosen fundamental belief is one we have chosen from the smorgasbord of beliefs we have come upon. Or we may just continue to live within the fundamental belief within which we were raised, perhaps without even articulating what it is and not actually exercise our right at the Adult Layer. This would have us acting as if the Teen Layer is the highest layer: giving priority to exercising our ability and right of individual free choice without having thought things through and very self-consciously chosen a fundamental belief to give priority.

In our behavior we are always doing one thing rather than another. Therefore we are always operating on a fundamental assumption about reality whether or not we are aware of what it is. Up until the Adult Layer, fundamentally it is usually that the universe is an immense number of separate parts and we are only the part of it that is our physical body. Thus when we very self-consciously think things through we usually choose a fundamental belief within this fundamental assumption. Some examples are "my purpose is to be personally happy," "my job is to do what Jesus, Muhammad, Buddha or another would want me to do," "personal fulfillment lies in being a good father or mother," "competition is the fundamental process in nature and happiness begins with finding financial success in a capitalist economy," or "happiness lies in loving my neighbor as myself."

Note something important at this point: it is our unconsciously or self-consciously chosen *priority* that determines the layer of maturity in the skill of self-consciousness. At the Baby Layer our priority is our *sensations*. At the Toddler Layer it is our *fundamental feeling of happy–not happy*. At the Child Layer it is our *wants*. At the Teen Layer it is our ability and right to exercise *free choice*. We continue *habitually* exercising all of them at the same time, being aware of our sensations, feelings, wants, and ability and right to exercise free choice. However, if we are giving priority to the latter with the former now all being habits, we are acting in full maturity at the Teen Layer of maturity. If we have very self-consciously chosen our fundamental belief and give it priority while at the same time doing all the others as habits, we are operating at the Adult Layer.

Our usual priority *visible in our behavior* reveals the layer of maturity we have mastered in the skill of self-consciousness. Thus at any time we are able to study *our usual behavior priority, not our intention,* to determine the layer of maturity at which we are currently and habitually operating in our lives. At the Adult Layer we have very self-consciously thought things through and chosen our fundamental belief. Now we give it priority at all times, or at least as much as we are able to do so.

ELDER

The next layer is the "Elder Layer." This is where we discover the *accurate fundamental belief.* It is that the universe is an indivisible whole.

It is also where we discover the importance of keeping our power, all of it, and using it to study our direct experience to determine if the universe is an immense number of separate parts or one indivisible whole, fundamentally the only two possibilities.

We do this because we now realize we have been living in partial freedom in the belief it is full freedom. We have been choosing our fundamental belief from the smorgasbord of beliefs we come upon and give our power to it. We also realize that this has our second priority be to obey it. We have *unconsciously* sustained the parent-child pattern of our childhood.

It is at the Elder Layer that we discover there is only one way to stop doing this and achieve true full freedom. *We have to give priority to studying our direct experience to determine our most fundamental belief.* We realize that when discovered there we can in any moment turn our attention to our experience and confirm it is accurate. The result is we have kept our power, all of it, and are now living in full freedom.

We no longer need to check with a second thing, a belief, before we can make a choice or act.

Lastly, it is where we discover how to practically integrate into our behavior the third of the three dimensions of self-consciousness: the *oneness of nature.* The other two were the *recognition of differences* (Toddler Layer) and the *mutual creation of a human language based on the illusion that there are separate parts (time and space) so we can be self-conscious* (Child Layer).

The main way we integrate the oneness of nature into our behavior is to become aware of the layers of maturity of the skill of self-consciousness and then elder ourselves into the mastery of the skill of each layer in the natural progression to where we have mastered the full skill.

As you will see as you read further, the pattern of thinking that represents the oneness of nature is to give priority to priorities. The most important set of priorities is the layers of maturity of the skill of self-consciousness. By mastering as a skill each layer in the natural progression we are integrating into our behavior and habits the three dimensions of the skill of self-consciousness that allows us to *both be self-conscious and happy.* Now our choice of actions are in alignment with reality.

In my judgment most societies on Earth are in transition from the Adult Layer to the Elder Layer. Up to the Adult Layer we are self-consciously or unconsciously operating on the assumption that the universe is, like the words in a language, an immense number of separate parts and we are one of them. At the Elder Layer we discover the opposite is true. As a result we realize we will need to make changes in almost every part of our behavior.

The main ones will be described in this section.

Ultimately Common Good Capitalism Necessitates Knowing the Elder Layer

Although a Common Good Capitalism Movement can emerge and be successful solely to end duopoly monopolies, it will not easily sustain success unless it becomes based on a maturation into the Elder Layer. Therefore, here is the most important point I am making in this book and why I am presenting the layers of maturity in it:

Common Good Capitalism will only be easily sustained by the thinking of those who have achieved the Elder Layer of maturity in the skill of self-consciousness. Other than a way to end duopoly monopolies it will not make sense to those still operating as if the Adult Layer or a lower layer is the highest layer of maturity in the skill of self-consciousness. Allow me to explain why I think this is true.

Money is something we have mutually created that can be exchanged for anything. Unlike barter where one specific thing has to be exchanged for another specific thing, such as a chicken for some vegetables, money can be exchanged for anything. In a village of a hundred people where everyone knows everyone else and all believe it is wise to give priority to their self-interest (Adult Layer or lower), a few people are going to end up with a lot of the money at the expense of everyone else. They will focus their attention on making a lot of money whereas most will give priority to something else such as falling in love, having and caring for their children, the arts, science, scholarship, or being of service to others.

As mentioned earlier, when people join to form a group they are making an agreement to give priority to the common good of it. Thus in this village there are only two ways for the villagers to consistently behave in ways that give priority to the common good:

1. creating laws that punish people for not doing so, or
2. people maturing to where they freely choose to give priority to the

common good because they discover it is where they find personal and social happiness in their lives.

In the book *The Big Short* by Michael Lewis and the movie by the same name, the limits of a system of laws to accomplish this goal are clearly revealed. The priority of each person is to find ways of getting around the laws to get more for one's self. Looked at from this point of view it is obvious that it will not be easy to create and enforce laws that are out in front of this process.

As is clearly revealed in the book and movie, the widespread belief that people will always pay their mortgages because in the past to a very high percentage they have was used to sell people bonds with good returns backed by mortgages. The demand for these bonds then became so great that to supply this demand some people made fees providing mortgages sold to people who had little ability to pay them. They bought houses, more than one, in the belief they could soon resell them (flip them) at a higher price because of another widespread belief that the prices of homes continually rise. The two rating agencies, Standard and Poor's and Moody's (a near triopoly monopoly with Fitch), both wanted the business of the banks selling the bonds so they gave the bonds high ratings when they knew that many of the mortgages backing them were not owned by people with sufficient income to support them if they couldn't quickly sell them. Finally, the people in the government regulatory agencies were giving priority to their career advancement that mainly laid in getting a higher paying job in the private sector. So to maintain good relationships with the people in the private sector banks they did not dig deep into discovering what was going on to protect the public.

When you add to this our ability today of having quick and easy access to nearly all information, it is clear that self-interested people will always find places where the law makers have not yet made laws to take advantage of "legal" opportunities for their self-interest, often and probably always at the expense of others.

This is the world we live in today. Only now, as *The Big Short* revealed, our village is a global village and giving priority to self-interest instead of the common good can result in global catastrophes like the Great Recession of 2008. This is also why they will continue to occur. This is also why companies have to continue to pursue becoming number one or two in their product markets because if they don't do it two other companies will achieve it. This is also why governments are letting these duopolies emerge: it is in the nations' self-interest to have their two duopolies conquer those product markets globally. Finally to support the developed nations significant head start in this process, there is strong support by them for free trade.

Fortunately people do not enjoy living at a lower layer of maturity in the skill of self-consciousness when they discover the next higher layer. Also, fortunately for most people in our global village society, the next higher layer is the Elder Layer. This is where people discover the greater joy of freely choosing to give priority to the common good and establishing relationships with others based on it.

It is discovered that we choose to embrace the Elder Layer for the same reason we always embrace each next layer of maturity of the skill of self-consciousness when discovered: moment-to-moment it is a more enjoyable way to live. And since there is no way the creation of laws can ever be out in front of all the ways people find to get around them, our next layer of more mature social agreements will be voluntary associations of people in the private sector.

This is common good capitalism. It is the natural and inevitable next layer of maturation of capitalism. It represents the priority of people who have matured into the Elder Layer of maturity of the skill of self-consciousness.

Also, fortunately, the duopolization of product markets makes this far easier to accomplish. Primarily only two companies in each product market need to voluntarily reach agreements that give priority to the common good while continuing to compete as their second priority. The smaller competitors will be invited to participate and join in the agreements or be exposed, mainly by the media and the companies who have joined in the agreement, as not doing so. The costs of not joining in such noble agreements could become so costly that they would conclude they have to join in the voluntary common good agreements to remain in business.

The Universe is an Indivisible Whole

Anything can be represented in words. There is also a fundamental way the universe operates. And it is also self-evident that each moment we are choosing one thing rather than another based on a self-consciously chosen or unconscious fundamental belief. Therefore, we can have some words represent our most fundamental belief.

As you will see as you read further, once this third dimension of the skill of self-consciousness is discovered, the oneness of nature, we need to also discover the accurate relationship between it and the mutual illusion tool of a human language (separate parts).

There are two possible directions from which we can discover that the universe is an indivisible whole. First we can come upon beliefs like those in many philosophies, religions, and sciences that assume it and decide it is going to be our most fundamental belief. Or we can become fed up, as I did, with everyone trying to get us to give them our power by joining them in their belief that I decided to keep it the only way it can be done. *I primarily went to my direct experience to discover my most fundamental belief.* I realized this is the only way I could keep my power, all of it, because I can then at any moment turn my attention to my immediate and direct experience to confirm it is accurate. This is what I did when I ended being on the path to become a Catholic priest.

As you will see explained in more details as you read further, the only way we can become a fully free human being is to keep our power and go to our direct experience to determine our most fundamental belief.

The Story of My Discovery That Oneness is a Fact

This is the story of the first time I discovered in direct experience that the universe is an indivisible whole.

A few years after college I was leaving a teaching position at Saint Leo College in Florida after a dramatic set of demonstrations that brought the national media to campus. We were the first college to have demonstrations in September of 1970 after the major college demonstrations during the previous school year.

The issue on our campus was allowing the boys to visit the girls in their dorms, not against the Vietnam War or on other national issues. Still all the national media—ABC, CBS, NBC, and Associated Press, Time, Newsweek—showed up because we were the first college unrest of the new school year. In the gymnasium I had played an important role in facilitating a peaceful resolution to the conflict by allowing the students to debate the issue and reach an agreement acceptable to all with the camera lights blaring on the entire student body of over 2,000 students, the faculty, and administrators. The conservative faculty thought it irresponsible that my facilitation did not allow for "adult input" and wanted to put me on trial. The president of the college offered my entire year's salary if I would leave and eliminate additional conflict so the campus could return to peace.

It was a major lesson for me. I knew it was right what I had done. Therefore, it was clear to me that I should defend my actions. At the same time I also knew it was more important to have the college return to peace. The chair of the board was running for governor of Florida, the election was a few weeks away, he was running on a law and order platform, and the president had informed me before the meeting of everyone in the gym that the chair was going to close the college if there was not a quick and peaceful solution that day. No one else but the president and I knew this. That was why, when chaos broke out and the camera lights went on, I had found the courage to offer to facilitate a process that was accepted by the students and resulted in a peaceful solution. The students in my classes had convinced the rest of the students to trust me to do it.

The President gave me a day to decide whether or not to leave the college or possibly sustain the disruption that could include the closing of the college by defending myself before the faculty court with the students being fully behind me.

That night, while walking back and forth along the shore of the pond near my trailer, I had concluded that it was more important to take the action that was best for all than standing on and defending a principle, that the students had the right to make the decision themselves. So I accepted the president's offer and resigned.

This was a very difficult decision for me. It was the first time I was aware of making a decision based on giving priority to the common good over defending a principle, the principle of justice. Instead of standing up for myself in the face of injustice as was my right and responsibility, I was allowing some other idea to trump it: the common good. I did not like the choice, but intuitively I knew it was the right thing to do.

Soon I was driving through the Great Smoky Mountains of Georgia on my way to joining my friend Jack Canfield in the doctoral program at the School of Education at the University of Massachusetts. At the time it was the best place to study humanistic psychology and I wanted to be trained to be a psychotherapist.

I was full of the intensity of this dramatic experience I had just had. The rain and fog clouds filled the forests, the car, and me in an equally dramatic way. I decided I needed to stop and take a moment to directly enjoy the stunning beauty of the moment.

I parked my car and walked up and over some rocks and out of view of the highway. There I found a large light brown flat rock sticking out from the mountain I could sit on. It allowed me to look down into the two valleys coming together at what looked like a mile down from me. Two rivers were flowing together and the near black looking wet pines filled the sides of the mountains all the way up to me. From this high vantage point I was able to see fog clouds move in and through the scene. Then it began to rain again.

I got up, took off all of my clothes, and put them under a rock where they would not get wet. I loved being raw in nature. In August, a couple of months before and on the drive down to Florida from Chicago to accept the teaching position at Saint Leo, one night I had slept on some rocks only inches above a flowing stream with only a sheet around me. So the idea of sitting naked while the rain pounded my body was something I was looking forward to experiencing.

The rain began to come down in buckets. I laid back on the large flat light brown rock and let it pound and message my full body. It felt like the immediate dramatic past in Florida was being washed away. For many minutes I laid there letting it massage me until it stopped.

When I sat back up I found myself confronted with a question.

Should I try saying the word "God" as if He, She, or It is real and see what the experience is in my body when I do it? I had thrown out the assumption that there is a God with all my other beliefs years earlier when I had decided to primarily go to my direct experience to find truths. I now found myself wanting to see if I could have a direct experience of God being real and feel it in my body.

This would be going to my direct experience to see if God is real.

I decided this was a good idea.

So I sat with my back straight and legs crossed. I was clear that "I" was not going to say the word "God" as if it was real. I was only going to allow my body to say it. It had to come from my body *experiencing* it as true to say the word "God" as if it is real.

I witnessed the feeling build inside me. I was very clear that I was not going to speak the word. I was only going to allow my body to speak the word when it felt truthful to do it.

I watched as the experience of a building up toward saying the word "God" as if real was occurring in my body to the point where only my body would speak the word "God" out loud as if it is real. The moment came when it spoke the word as if God was real.

At that very instant the world blew up! There was extremely loud thunder and lightning, the thunder rolling on and on and the lightning screaming in sharp crackles. It was extremely loud and powerfully dramatic and lasted for nearly a minute.

I laughed at the coincidence. I was not so romantic that I added to the experience that something special had just happened to me, that I should found a church or something, or whatever can happen to one when things like this happen. I just laughed off the coincidence and went back to doing what I was doing.

Again, I watched what felt like a building inside my body to say the word "God" as if it was identifying something that is real. I was very clear that I was not by choice going to speak the word. Only my body could speak the word when it felt right to do it…when it felt it was representing an experience that was real.

I again watched as the experience of a building up toward saying the word "God" as if it were real was occurring in my body to the point where again only my body eventually spoke the word "God" out loud as if it is real.

At that exact instant the world blew up again! There was extremely loud thunder and lightning, the thunder rolling on and on and the lightning screamed many sharp crackles just as before. It was again extremely loud and powerfully dramatic for nearly a minute.

I suddenly realized what had happened.

The experience of a building of momentum to say the word God I was witnessing going on inside my body was the same building up of nature to pop out thunder and lightning.

Then this thought came to me to explain what I had just experienced: "Oneness is not an idea; it is a fact."

I realized that I had just had a direct and self-conscious experience of the oneness of nature.

I knew almost nothing of what you have read in this book. So I did not know what to do with this experience, much less how to make it active in my behavior. All I knew was that the universe is an indivisible whole, that is a fact, and I just had a direct and self-consciously known experience of it.

So, being the fun guy that I sometimes like to be, after digesting this delicious experience, I looked up at the gray clouds and said the word "God" loudly, and this time there was no thunder and lightning. I then shouted, "Gotcha!!!!" at nature and fell back laughing with great delight as I rolled around on the big flat brown rock in the great joy of my direct experience discovery.

From that day forward I knew that the universe is an indivisible whole and I was one of its parts that cannot be separated from it. I had no idea at the time that it would take me nearly a lifetime to understand how to live each moment as if this is true as a skill. That is why, now in my seventies, I have decided to write this book. My purpose is to shorten the time it will take you to master the full skill of self-consciousness both for your personal joy but also so we can mature capitalism into common good capitalism. Today it is one of the most powerful forces on Earth and, therefore, our maturation into common good capitalism is one of the best things we can do for the common good of our now global village.

A Guide to Discovering the Accurate Fundamental Inside Belief in Direct Experience

Allow me to now guide you into a study of your direct experience so you can identify your accurate relationship with nature. Then whatever you choose as your fundamental belief will accurately represent what you are actually doing when you are keeping your power and primarily relating directly with nature without an intermediary.

There are many ways people discover this truth and turn it into a skill. The above story revealed the way I first became aware in direct experience that oneness was a fact and not just a possible belief in words. What I will present below is what I believe is the way many people throughout history have discovered it.

Earlier, in the Introduction, I guided you through this series of observations. This time be extremely serious about it as you do it. It could result in your permanent maturation into the Elder Layer.

The first question that has probably most often been asked is this: "Is the air cooperating or competing with my lungs?" We have all heard of meditation practices where people are taught to focus on the air going in and out of their noses. One of the reasons throughout history people have been guided to do this is that it naturally leads to asking themselves the above question. When one studies this question the answer becomes self-evident and obvious: the air is consistently cooperating with our lungs. In fact, it has been doing so since we were born and will be effortlessly doing so until we die. Thus, we easily conclude cooperation, not competition, is the consistent and effortless relationship between the air and our lungs.

The next question becomes: "What is doing our breathing?" We have been naturally and effortlessly breathing since coming out of our mother's womb and will be doing so until we die. We do not self-consciously choose to do our breathing.

The first guess is usually "Our lungs are doing our breathing." However, if we take the lungs out of our physical bodies and put them on the table, they would not be able to do our breathing. So it becomes clear that it is more accurate to say, "Our physical bodies and lungs are doing our breathing." Without our physical bodies being alive our lungs would not be able to do our breathing.

It then becomes clear that without the air around us, we would not be able to do our breathing. So we conclude that it is more accurate to say, "The air, our physical bodies, and lungs are doing our breathing."

Then we realize that if the Earth had the atmosphere of Mars we would not be able to do our breathing. So we conclude that it is more accurate to say, "The Earth's atmosphere, the air around us, our physical bodies, and our lungs are doing our breathing." But then we realize that if the Earth was not in its particular relationship with the sun, our galaxy, and the rest of the universe we would not be able to do our breathing. This has us conclude that, in fact, the accurate answer is "It is the universe that is doing our breathing."

Allow me to suggest that, before reading the paragraph after this one, you set aside this book and take a few minutes to be aware that it is, indeed, the universe that is doing your breathing. Then watch your breath. Do not do anything to effect it. *Just watch it with the full awareness that it is the universe that is doing your breathing.* See what you notice. This book will still be here when you are done.

Below I will comment on what you probably experienced when you watched the universe doing your breathing. But first allow me to bring your attention to this.

If our lungs do not have air for two minutes, we will die. If our physical bodies cannot operate our lungs for two minutes, we will die. If the air is not available for two minutes, we will die. If the Earth is not surrounded with its atmosphere for two minutes, all things that breathe and us will die. If the Earth is not in the particular relationships it is in with the rest of the universe for two minutes, we will die.

Eventually it becomes obvious from a study of our direct experience that the indivisible universe is doing our breathing. There are no gaps between things and everything is connected, interdependent, and equally real. And if any one of these parts of the universe is not present and doing exactly what it is doing, we would not be able to breathe. Therefore, we conclude, the universe is an indivisible whole.

This is why when you watched your breathing within the awareness that the universe is doing it that you probably settled into a comfortable place of it being more full while also more relaxed and rhythmic. If we are each first the universe, there is nothing to fear. If there is nothing to fear, there is no reason to constrict our breathing. Some schools of medicine on Earth focus on making sure we are breathing in the above way to sustain health.

It is through observations like this in their here and now direct experience that has had people throughout history discover that the universe is an indivisible whole. Therefore, we conclude, we are first it that will not die and secondly our physical bodies that will die. Our hand knows itself as first the whole physical body and secondly itself. In the same way we come to know ourselves as first the whole universe and secondly our physical bodies. This also means that at full maturity in the skill of self-consciousness our natural and effortless priority is the common good. As best we are able and from wherever we are standing it is continuous participation in the maturation of the universe, the most fundamental process in nature.

By the way, lets focus on music and song for a moment. I suspect that originally it was the self-conscious experience together of the direct experience of oneness. We sing the same melody and words at the same time. Today we tend to divide it into performers and audience, but I doubt that that division was present when it was originally created and enjoyed.

Next we ask ourselves this question: "Are the parts of my body primarily cooperating with each other or primarily competing with each other?" Once again it becomes self-evident and obvious that, when we are healthy, they are consistently and effortlessly cooperating with each other. Our right hand has never gotten into a fight with our left hand. Once again it is self-evident and obvious that our liver, stomach, knees, arms, legs, lungs, fingernails, hair, and all the parts of our body are in a consistent pattern of cooperation with each other with the priority being the health of our whole physical body.

Next we turn our attention to nature and ask ourselves this question: "Is the air, water, sun, and dirt primarily competing or cooperating with each other?" Once again it becomes obvious that they are primarily and consistently cooperating to grow the plants we need to survive. Two plants next to each other may compete for the sun, but that is secondary. Fundamentally they are all cooperating with each other to grow the plants we need to eat to survive.

The next questions become: "What is cooperation?" and "What is competition?" The answer to the first question also becomes obvious. *Cooperation is when the parts give priority to the whole.* The parts of our physical bodies are giving priority to the health of our physical bodies. The air going in and out of our lungs and the parts of our physical bodies are giving priority to the health of our physical bodies. And the air, water, sun, and dirt are giving priority to the health of nature and the universe. This has one conclude that cooperation is the fundamental process in nature.

Competition, on the other hand, is when a part gives priority to itself in relationship with the other parts. More about this below.

Once it becomes obvious that cooperation, not competition, is the fundamental process in nature it also becomes obvious that the universe is a whole, an indivisible whole. It is one thing, not an immense number of separate parts as are the words in a language.

From our study of our direct experience we discover that since we learned a language we have been unconsciously operating as if the fundamental assumption in language is also the accurate fundamental assumption in nature.

When we learned a language as a small child we unconsciously took on the fundamental assumption in language as the fundamental assumption in nature. We now know it is not. However we can now also see that acting as if it is real was a very valuable *mutually agreed upon illusion tool*: it allowed us to create our human language and that, in turn, allowed us to be self-conscious.

Therefore, this mutually agreed upon illusion tool is a very valuable one. However it is still an illusion, something not true. It is a *tool —a mutually created tool*—we created to become self-conscious.

Next we realize that if cooperation is the fundamental process in nature then it is inescapable. This means that competition must be a kind of cooperation.

In a language it is the opposite of cooperation, but in reality it only exists as a kind of cooperation.

Cooperation is the fundamental process in nature, it cannot be escaped, and in nature there is no opposite of it. It turns out that, just like compromise, agreement, and love, *competition is a form of cooperation, the lowest of these forms.*

As I pointed out to the corporate leaders at Davos, if I have an apple in my hand and neither you or I want it, anyone can take it and we would both be as happy afterwards as we were before. However it we both want the apple we could compete over it. Notice as I pointed out to them, without the cooperative agreement that we both want the apple the competition would not be possible.

The point is that competition cannot occur except in a cooperative context. It is a form of cooperation.

In language it can be an opposite. However in nature it does not exist accept as secondary in importance, as a way of cooperating. *Compromise* is a more mature form of cooperation. *Agreement* is an even more mature form of cooperation, and *love*—freely choosing to self-consciously move as one with each other and nature—is the most mature form of cooperation.

The result of this keeping of one's power and using it to study one's immediate and direct experience ultimately leads to the discovery of what is self-evident and obvious: the universe is one indivisible whole because all of its parts consistently give priority to the health and maturation of the one whole.

Opposites Only Exist in Language

The idea that competition is the fundamental process in nature as so many of us were taught in school is inaccurate. It is the result of people unaware that they are still operating as if the fundamental assumption in language is the accurate fundamental assumption about reality.

In language the basic structure is opposites: black-white, up-down, high-low...or in the case of the universe, oneness-separate parts. Since oneness and separate parts are clearly opposites it is believed one of them must be real and the other false, an illusion.

As we just discovered by observing our direct experience, it is self-evident that the universe is an indivisible whole (oneness). Separate parts, we then realize, only exist in language. They do not exist in reality. Oneness does not have an opposite in reality, only in a language.

Not being aware that language is always between them and what they are thinking or perceiving because it is what allows them to be self-conscious, *they have unconsciously projected opposites into their observation of reality.*

More important, they have failed to see that whereas they are opposites in language both oneness and separate parts are *equally valuable* even though in language one represents reality and the other represents an illusion.

There are no opposites in reality. As we just observed it is self-evident that the universe is an indivisible whole. At the same time the perception of time and space (separate parts) is *equally valuable*: it allows us to be self-conscious parts of the universe, to think about the past, plan for the future, and consistently execute our plan in the present.

I repeat: opposites only exist in language; they do not exist in reality. The universe is an indivisible whole and the mutual illusion tool of a human language is equally valuable: it allows us to be self-conscious.

Unaware a human language is always between them and what they are observing they have tended to believe it necessary to assume one of them real and the other not. They have usually concluded that separate parts (time and space) are real and oneness is an illusion. The truth is the opposite. Oneness is real and separate parts (time and space) are an illusion. However they are both *equally valuable!* The illusion of separate parts is a very valuable *mutual illusion tool*: it allows us to be self-conscious.

As has been done by individuals and communities throughout history, all one has to do to discover this is true is to keep one's power and use it to study one's immediate and direct experience as we have just done and then figure out what must be the relationship between the oneness of nature and languages.

Next we ask ourselves this question: "Does the universe die?" Again it is obvious that there is no evidence that the universe will ever die. We will die. This we know to be true. However we can find no evidence that the universe will ever die.

Even if we turn our attention to what the scientists have discovered it becomes clear that no one has found the beginning, end, or edge of the universe. We have theories like the Big Bang Theory, but I loved the moment I witnessed on a science show on television when a scientist was asked, "What came before the Big Bang?" The person answered, "Probably another Big Bang." In other words, the Big Bang Theory may be a theory of how the universe became the way it is today but it has not answered the question, "What was the beginning of the universe?" We also cannot see beyond the light horizon (as far as light will allow us to see). Therefore we have not found an edge to the universe.

My point is a simple one. Thus far we have no evidence of the universe having a beginning, end, or edge. We do not yet understand how this can be the case, but at some point in the future I trust we probably will. However at this point it is obvious that there is no evidence that the universe will ever die.

It is at this point that people throughout history have realized that their accurate self-definition is: "I am first the universe that will not die and secondly my physical body that will die." It is this conclusion that has naturally led people to choose moral behavior as their primary habit: freely choosing to give priority to the common good of us all.

Moral behavior is the natural priority at the Elder Layer of maturity in the skill of self-consciousness.

As mentioned earlier, most of us in the developed nations have been brought up to believe that competition is the fundamental process in nature. If this is not true, how could this inaccurate fundamental belief have been so easily sustained even up to now? Understanding the layers of maturity of the skill of self-consciousness can help us understand how this occurred.

Throughout most of history and up to now human societies have often been operating on the assumption that the Adult Layer or one of the lower layers of maturity of the skill of self-consciousness is the highest layer. As a result we were unaware that we were sustaining the pattern of *voluntary unconscious oppression*. That is, we thought it wise to give our power to another, another person or a belief. So tribes usually had chiefs, a father substitute, and the pattern of the Toddler-Child Layers of maturity were sustained as if they were the highest layers. Nations had kings and queens. Some, it was believed, even had a direct line to God we did not have.

This deep paternal pattern only began to be replaced by democracy as a result of the emergence of science. The basic assumption in science is that we can discover truths of how the universe is working from studying our direct experiences. A ball of a certain size will travel at the same speed every time it rolls down a flat board at a certain angle. The result was that we no longer needed the king or queen's direct line to God to know truths.

More important, with the king or queen no longer needed we were each free to exercise our ability and right of free choice.

This ultimately resulted in activities like the Pilgrims sailing to America and creating the first nation that has been sustained as a democracy. This was an example of a *mutual honoring* of maturation into the Teen Layer of maturity in the skill of self-consciousness. As mentioned earlier, today two-thirds of the nations on Earth are democracies and those of us living in them are confident that eventually all nations will be democracies. We feel as confident in this judgment as our judgment that a baby will learn to walk and speak a language: we know there are layers of maturity of the skill of self-consciousness and that the Teen Layer is one of them.

However *unconscious voluntary oppression* is a deep unconscious pattern. We have become fully aware of outside oppression and are very diligent about making sure we do not regress back into it. However many are still not aware of the voluntary unconscious oppression that still lives inside them. As a result they are still giving their power to a second thing that does not exist, a belief.

If the universe is an indivisible whole, there is not a second thing to receive our power.

Unaware that they are assuming that the universe is an immense number of separate parts and they are each one of them, they are unconsciously sustaining the childhood pattern of giving their power to a father-mother substitute, today usually a belief.

Allow me to now describe the changes in our thinking and behavior that will eventually occur once this is known and the discovery in direct experience that the universe is an indivisible whole has occurred.

Allow me to emphasize again that only those who discover this and make these changes will find it natural to graduate their economic activity into being one of the pioneers of common good capitalism. At the Adult Layer or lower they will easily conclude that it makes sense to give priority to the self-interest of their physical body. They will still be assuming it is natural and mature to do so. They may participate in a movement to end duopoly monopolies but they will not easily sustain common good capitalism in its place.

Even though this presentation is not in the languages of economics and business these layers of maturity need to be presented in this book. It is only at the Elder Layer that one's self-definition and primary self-interest change to where it is experienced as natural to give priority to the common good.

Partial Freedom and Full Freedom

It is at the Elder Layer, as a result of the discovery that the universe is an indivisible whole, that we realize there is not a second thing to receive our power. Therefore we give priority to keeping our power and using it to study our immediate and direct experience to identify our most fundamental belief. Doing this reveals that we have been operating in partial freedom and believing we were in full freedom. We now end choosing our fundamental belief from the smorgasbord of beliefs (partial freedom) and solely choose it from a study of our immediate and direct experience (full freedom).

More on Outside and Inside Oppression

As described earlier, it is self-evident that *from the inside* no one else can move our arms and legs or think our thoughts. And *from the inside* none of us can do this for anyone else. Thus, by nature, we are each a fully free human being. We have the ability and right to choose our actions. We are, therefore, also fully responsible for those actions.

When we are not allowed to exercise this ability and right of free choice, it is called "oppression." We are all familiar with *outside oppression*.

We grow up inside a family structure that, for our protection when young, establishes rules we must follow, everything from saying "thank you" to being home "before midnight." Our parents gradually release the rules as we become capable of exercising our ability, right, and skill of individual freedom responsibility, that is, within the rules of the family and society within which we live. At the Adult Layer of maturity we are usually fully free of parental oversight. And, aside from an obligation to obey the rules of the society within which we live, we are free to exercise our ability and right of individual freedom.

We are free of outside oppression.

However, as described earlier, there are two forms of oppression: *outside oppression* and *inside oppression*. It is at the Elder Layer that we discover how to become free of inside oppression.

Inside oppression is when we voluntarily give priority to another person or a belief and then obey him, her, or it.

Thus, the Elder Layer is when we discover that we have to give priority to the fundamental belief we discover to be accurate in our direct experience. It is here that we discover the only thing we could give priority that is not a second thing: *our direct experience.*

Outside and Inside Beliefs

In our thinking there are two kinds of beliefs: outside and inside beliefs.

Outside beliefs are beliefs we have chosen from the smorgasbord of beliefs we come upon in life and they will surely mature as we move through life. *We give our power to them and our second priority is to obey them.* Regarding our most fundamental outside belief, we make sure that all our other beliefs, choices, and actions are consistently in alignment with it.

This is our priority at the Adult Layer of maturity in the skill of self-consciousness.

Inside beliefs are the beliefs we have chosen primarily as the result of a study of our direct experience. Here we keep our power, all of it, and primarily use it to determine our fundamental belief from a study of our immediate and direct experience. Now we can at any time again turn our attention to witness that it is true. *Our priority is our direct experience,* and as a result we have sustained our ability to exercise free choice now and in the future. *Our second priority is the formation of a belief in words* so we can talk about it with others and ourselves.

Choosing an inside belief as our fundamental belief is our priority at the Elder Layer.

Thus, our most fundamental *outside belief* is a belief we have chosen from the beliefs we have come upon in life, we give our power to it, and our second priority is to obey it. An *inside belief* is second in importance to our ability to turn our attention at any moment to our immediate and direct experience and observe that what we have represented in words as an inside belief is accurate.

Here the direct experience is the priority, not the words.

We have kept our power, ended *voluntary inside oppression,* and are living a fully free life. We no longer need to check with a second party, an outside belief, before we can act. Also, this inside belief also becomes a *knowledge skill.* Like the knowledge skill that the best way to walk through a wall is where there is a door, the direct experience that the universe is an indivisible whole is a knowledge skill. Therefore it is now always present in our thinking or being mastered as a habit to be always present in our thinking.

Personal Science

This writer calls this activity "personal science." This is to distinguish it from "professional science."

Professional science is the study of experience to identify truths and then share them with the rest of us. *Personal science* is each of us primarily turning our attention to our immediate direct experience to identify our most fundamental inside belief. This is keeping our power and using it to be a fully free rather than partially free human being. Only by doing this are we not giving our power to a second thing.

Professional science is discovering truths. Personal science is becoming truth.

When we came into the world as a baby and for the first many years of our lives, we were fully dependent upon others for survival. So we are in a deep pattern of giving our power to something outside our physical bodies to survive and mature.

So it is easy to unconsciously continue to do this by giving our power to a freely chosen outside belief.

Today it is professional science that is often in the parent role. If we learn in the news that scientific studies prove that eating avocados will have us all lose weight to where the men will look like Brad Pitt and the women will look like Jennifer Lopez, the next day all grocery stores will sell out of avocados.

Professional science is very valuable. However, to achieve full maturity in the skill of self-consciousness we each need to keep our power. We each need to end this unconscious pattern of primarily giving our power to a second thing because we now know a second thing to receive it does not exist: the universe is an indivisible whole. At the Elder Layer we discover how to end this inaccurate unconscious pattern.

We have to primarily be personal scientists.

We also must conclude from this activity that the universe is an indivisible whole because it is. If not, by default we will be giving priority, and our power, to a belief (Adult Layer), one we have freely chosen or unconsciously grew up inside and still honor.

We will still be in partial freedom in the belief that we are in full freedom.

Thus I trust you now understand why in writing this book I am not justifying anything based on an authority. At the Elder Layer we understand the importance of ending primarily giving our power to any second thing, *either outside our physical bodies or inside us to an outside belief in our thinking.* The first is allowing outside oppression and the second, without intending to do so, is allowing inside oppression. We have only achieved maturity in the skill of self-consciousness at the Elder Layer when we determine our fundamental inside belief *primarily* from a study of immediate direct experience.

Then and only then are we fully free human beings on the inside and as well, hopefully, on the outside. We now also know that true full freedom is a skill, not a belief. It is the skill of being a personal scientist.

Language is a Mutually Agreed Upon Illusion Tool

To understand the difference between partial freedom and full freedom it is helpful to understand the relationship between a human language and the oneness of nature.

It is at this layer that we discover that since we learned a language at two years old we have been operating as if the fundamental assumption in language is the accurate fundamental assumption about reality: that the universe, like the words in a human language, is an immense number of separate parts. We now know it is an indivisible whole. Therefore, we now know that the fundamental assumption that allows us to create a human language, that the universe is separate parts like words, is not true. It is a *mutually agreed upon illusion tool* that allows us to create words to identify one thing as different from another and be able to have another person know which one we are talking about. Our human languages are, therefore, very valuable. They also, in turn, allow us to be self-conscious, to know what we are doing while we are doing it, to analyze the past, plan for the future, and consistently execute our plan in the present. It also allows us the ability to choose our self-definition.

There are over 6,000 human languages on Earth. To create a human language, by agreement we had to give a sound and symbol to each thing, such as "table" and "chair," so others would know which one we were talking about. This was only possible when we created the assumption that there are separate parts (time and space). This assumption is not accurate but it is a very valuable *mutual illusion tool* we created that allows us to create a human language. This in turn allows us to become self-conscious.

So this mutual illusion tool called "separate parts" or "time and space" is as valuable as the oneness of nature: it allows the indivisible universe to be self-conscious through its human parts.

However, since it is an illusion and oneness is reality, below we will learn that it is essential that we learn how to give *priority* to the oneness of nature and second priority to this *equally valuable* mutually agreed upon illusion called "human languages" that allow us to be self-conscious parts of the indivisible universe. We do not polarize them and make one good and the other bad. *They are both equally valuable.* Therefore, instead of polarizing them we prioritize them and are able to simultaneously do both easily because we give priority to oneness (reality) and second priority to human languages (our mutually created human illusion tool).

Full Freedom is a Skill

When we learn any skill we also create inside beliefs. For instance, when we learn to ride a bicycle, our priority is the mastery of the skill in our immediate and direct experience. Only secondly do we form some beliefs about how to ride a bicycle, for instance, "we maintain balance by peddling or gliding." The priority in our thinking is the *skill experience* and the beliefs we form about it are secondary in importance. They are inside beliefs.

We are always unconsciously or self-consciously operating on a fundamental belief about reality. It is determining each of our choices to do one thing rather than another. We may not be able to say in words what it is, but it is always there. *By default* it is the fundamental assumption we *unconsciously* began to operate on when we learned a language: that the universe like the words in a language is an immense number of separate parts.

The Elder Layer of maturity is when we discover that up to now we have unconsciously been doing this and choose to end this voluntary inside oppression. We do this by ending the giving of priority to any outside belief and, instead, turn our attention to mastering true individual freedom as a skill by primarily studying our direct experience to identify our fundamental inside belief. This is the knowledge skill of the Elder Layer.

If the society within which we live operates in ignorance of this, we could remain at the Adult Layer (priority in an outside belief) as if it is the highest layer of maturity possible in the skill of self-consciousness the rest of our lives. However if we live in a society that is fully aware of the importance of mastering as skills all the layers of maturity of the skill of self-consciousness, it will give highest priority to the eldering of its children up the layers to full maturity before they are in their twenties. They will know that nothing is more important both for the personal happiness of each child and the happiness of the community.

They will know that the *skill of self-consciousness* is a skill to be learned. Like any skill there are layers of smaller skills in the learning of it. No layer can be skipped. And, therefore, they must be learned in the natural progression.

The mastery of a skill is always the mastery of the relationship between what we are doing and nature to move as a cooperative activity between the two. When it then becomes a habit it can be an activity not always in need of our direct attention. We could simultaneously be riding a bicycle, using a hammer to pound a nail, or driving an automobile.

It is the same with the mastery of the *human skill of self-consciousness.* There are layers of small skills of mastering this skill and we want to turn the skill of each layer into habits so we can enjoy the mastery of the full skill of self-consciousness as a habit.

The Three Aspects of the Skill of Self-Consciousness

There are three aspects to the skill of self-consciousness: the content, context, and process. At the Elder Layer we correctly identify all three.

The *accurate content* is the accurate fundamental inside belief: the universe is an indivisible whole.

The *accurate context* is the accurate self-definition: "I am first the universe that will not die and secondly my physical body that will die."

The *accurate process* is the giving of priority to the pattern of thinking that assumes oneness is a fact: giving priority to priorities.

Allow me to now explain a bit more about each.

The Accurate Fundamental Belief is
That the Universe is an Indivisible Whole

We earlier discovered the accurate fundamental inside belief by doing what people throughout history have done. We discovered we were unconsciously and voluntarily experiencing the pain of inside oppression. We were giving our power to a second thing, another person or outside belief, and didn't have it anymore. That was painful. Then by keeping our power, all of it, and using it to study our immediate and direct experience of our breathing we were able to determine that the universe is an indivisible whole and that, therefore, cooperation is the fundamental process in nature. Then, as we will soon do, by studying the changes of the behavior of others and our own over time that maturation is the particular kind of cooperation that is the fundamental process in nature.

The Accurate Self-Definition then is "I am first the universe that will not die and secondly my physical body that will die."

If the universe is an indivisible whole that will not die, then it is clear that we are first it and only secondly our physical bodies, the only part of the universe over which we have sole and full inside control, that will die. So not only do we need to choose the above as our fundamental inside belief but we also have to change to have the above self-definition be our new self-definition that honors this truth.

This is the natural source of moral behavior throughout history.

We naturally mature to where we understand that our priority is not our physical body. Our priority becomes whatever we can each do each moment that is the best unique thing (no one else is ever standing where we are standing) for the common good of the universe, our true total self.

The Accurate Primary Pattern of Thinking, the Giving of Priority to Priorities

Up to the Adult Layer of maturity we use the pattern of thinking that assumes separate parts are real. That pattern is "choosing between this or that in time and space." In our thinking it is the coatrack upon which we hang all of our thoughts.

At the Elder Layer we realize we need to also change the coatrack, the assumption behind our pattern of thinking. We need to find the pattern of thinking—the wordrack—that represents the oneness of nature.

When we are assuming separate parts (time and space) are real, our thinking is in the pattern of "this-or-that in time and space as if they are real." To get an apple it takes time to go from being in the living room to being in the kitchen. This describes two spaces and some time to go from one to the other.

However it does not take time to go from being our left hand to being our right hand: we already know them as parts of the whole we label our physical body.

Inside our skin is where we are familiar with using the pattern of thinking of oneness.

It is the place where we currently assume it does not take time to go from one location to another because we already define "self" as all of the locations. Here we think of ourselves as first our whole body and only secondly one or any of its parts. If we get in an automobile accident and it is necessary to remove a leg to survive, we give priority to saving the whole body over saving the leg.

This oneness pattern of thinking is giving priority to priorities. There are no factors of time and space (the assumption of separate parts) when thinking in the pattern of priorities. Priorities exist in all time and all space (oneness). The words for each are only present so we can be self-consciously aware they are in all time and all space.

Thus, this is the pattern of thinking that represents the assumption that the universe is an indivisible whole. It explains why, throughout nearly all of history, "moral behavior" has been defined as "freely choosing to give *priority* to the common good." The oneness pattern of thinking is used.

For instance, at each layer of maturity in the skill of self-consciousness we do not give up the skill we learned at each lower layer. We just give priority to the skill of the layer of maturity we are on, for instance the Adult Layer, and second priority to each of the lower layers as we learned them. Our second priority is our ability and right of individual freedom (Teen Layer). Our third priority is our wants (Child Layer). Our fourth priority is our fundamental feeling of happy-not happy (Toddler Layer). And our fifth priority is our sensations, the experience of being alive (Baby Layer).

Once we discover this we immediately realize that we do not want to give up the separate parts pattern of thinking. It allows us to create and use a human language that in turn allows us to be self-conscious. So what we immediately realize is that we will now simultaneously use both patterns of thinking and give priority to the oneness pattern of thinking because it accurately represents reality. This is using the priority pattern of thinking to organize in our thinking the relationship between the two possible fundamental patterns of thinking.

As described in the Introduction, using both patterns of thinking simultaneously is the equivalent of playing the piano with two hands instead of one hand. The Child to Adult Layers is the equivalent of only using the right hand to pluck out a melody. When we simultaneously use both patterns of thinking it is the equivalent of using both hands to play the piano. The left hand plays a rhythm, the same pattern repeatedly. This is the equivalent of the oneness pattern of thinking. The right hand continues to play the melody. This is the equivalent of the separate parts pattern of thinking. While doing both fully at the same time, the melody (the differentiated part) always gives priority to the rhythm (oneness) in the same way at the Elder Layer our separate parts pattern of thinking always gives priority to the oneness pattern of thinking. Primarily using this knowledge discovered in direct experience is the thinking skill of the Elder Layer.

At the Elder Layer we master the skill of self-consciously and simultaneously using both patterns of thinking and always give priority to the oneness pattern of thinking, the giving of priority to priorities. Our most fundamental priority pattern is giving priority to being the universe that will not die (oneness) and second priority to being our physical body that will die (a separate part). Primarily using this knowledge discovered in direct experience is the knowledge skill of the Elder Layer.

Maturation is the Particular Kind of Cooperation that is the Fundamental Process in Nature

It is also obvious that maturation is the *particular kind of cooperation* that is the fundamental process in nature.

As already pointed out a couple of times, when we learn to walk we do not go back to crawling. When we learn to ride a bicycle, we consistently ride it without falling down. When we learn to use chopsticks with one hand we stop using them with two hands. It is quite obvious that maturation is the particular kind of cooperation that is the fundamental process in nature.

We can look at children and see that they all mature up the lower layers of maturity of the skill of self-consciousness. We can notice that we have as well. When we mature into the Teen Layer we choose democracy and do not go back to choosing dictatorship.

The lower layers are now common knowledge and, therefore, all in our societies elder us into proficiency in the skills of those layers. It is the highest two layers that are not yet common knowledge. However someday they surely will be.

Cooperation describes a process. It does not describe why the process is occurring.

From a study of our direct experiences we can witness that maturation is the particular kind of cooperation that is always occurring.

Maturation is *why* the cooperation is occurring.

It is not only the maturation of parts of the universe, such as us. If the universe is an indivisible whole, then anything occurring in the mutually agreed upon illusion of separate parts (time and space) is secondary in importance. *Primarily* it is always the indivisible universe that is maturing.

Maturation is not something that *primarily* exists in time and space. There was a moment when I did not know how to ride a bicycle and then a later moment when I did. It takes time to learn a skill. However having a skill and not having a skill is not itself something in time and space. It is a difference, but it is a difference in maturation, not in something happening over a period of time. We now know something or can do a skill that we use to not be able to do. The knowing of it and not knowing of it are two layers of maturity. Everything else is the same. We just know something we previously did not know that allows us to relate with the universe differently. This knowing something relative to not knowing it is perceived as different layers of maturity. There are not factors of time and space (separate parts) in layers of maturity. They exist in all time and all space. The fact that it took time to master the skill is secondary in importance.

The parts mature and also decay. It is always the universe that is primarily maturing and as a whole it does not decay. It changes but, as Albert Einstein discovered, energy can neither be created nor destroyed. What we also know is that it, the universe, matures.

While our physical bodies will decay, we can be participating in the fundamental process of maturation up until our last breath. The Elder Layer of maturity in the skill of self-consciousness allows us to know that we are first the universe that will not die and only secondly our physical bodies that do die and that the universe is always in a constant state of maturing.

Thus, whether or not we are aware of it, we are in a constant state of maturation, *or we are participating in maturation by choice.* As we get closer to death our physical bodies begin to decay but even until we breathe our last breath our priority is assisting others and our social agreements to mature.

What is self-evident is that once we know of a more mature way of being we prefer it to the less mature way of being. Therefore we naturally and effortlessly begin to master the more mature way of being as a skill and have it become a habit that replaces the old habit. This is true for us as individual human beings and in our agreements with each other, usually called "a society."

Therefore, the fundamental process in nature is not just a cooperative process; we are also going somewhere. Not primarily in the mutually agreed upon illusions of time and space but in maturation.

People living on Earth 2000 years ago could not have easily imagined electricity, computers, satellites, nuclear bombs, and a man walking on the moon. We have little idea of how human beings will be living together 2000 years in the future. What forms things will take in the definitions of time and space are not what is most important.

What is most important is that we know that the fundamental process in nature is maturation, a particular kind of cooperation. In all we do we can witness this as true each and every moment.

Observations like this in our direct experience result in our maturation into the Elder Layer. It is this and only this that will enable us to naturally and effortlessly make sure from this point forward that our highest priority is the common good, *direct self-conscious participation in maturation.*

The assumption that we should consider that the universe is an indivisible whole is at first a shock. The size of the universe is so large that this doesn't seem possible. But we eventually discover that what is most important here is not its size.

What is most important is the relationship among the parts of the universe.

Are they separate from one another or do they behave as fully connected to each other, interdependent, equally real, and unable to be separated from each other? When we put aside all the beliefs we grew up inside and solely give priority to our immediate direct experience, it is obvious that the relationship between and among the parts is indivisible.

No part of the universe can be separated from the rest of it and even if that were possible there is not a second place to put it.

It is not possible to separate the tree from the ground, water, and air and have it be a tree. It is not possible to separate you and me from food, water, and air and have us be human beings. The air is obviously cooperating with our lungs, not competing with them.

When we solely turn our attention to our immediate direct experience this is self-evident. However we also find it is not easy to put aside the other fact that most of us are living with each other *as if we are each only our physical bodies.*

That is a good thing! It is part of an essential layer of maturity in the mastery of the skill of self-consciousness (Child Layer). It is the assumption that separate parts exist that allows us to create our human languages and thereby become self-conscious parts of the universe.

It is a layer of maturity in the skill of self-consciousness we need to know before we can know the higher layers. However, as we have observed, the creation of separate parts is a *mutual illusion tool.* Therefore, while fully doing both, we need to learn to give priority to the truth. It is that the universe is an indivisible whole. We then give second priority to the use of this mutual illusion tool called "human languages," *which allows us to be self-conscious parts of the universe.* And even though they are opposites, one real (oneness) and one illusion (the assumption that separate parts exist) when priority is given to the one that is real and second priority to the mutually agreed upon illusion they are naturally and effortlessly in full cooperation with each other. This is the primary skill at the Elder Layer.

There is a wonderful thing about separate parts being an illusion: illusions are never a threat to reality and, as in art, can easily be in full cooperation with it. This allows an illusion, such as playing Hamlet on a stage, to easily be in full cooperation with reality, that the person, Joe Smith, is not Hamlet and everyone in the audience and on stage knows this is true. As a result Joe Smith is able to fully be both himself and Hamlet at the same time. However, if Joe Smith thought he was primarily Hamlet and secondly Joe Smith, he would clearly not be in a mature relationship with reality. It is only because he accurately knows which is real and which is an illusion that he can fully, easily, and simultaneously be both.

Illusion can be in full and easy cooperation with reality. Thus languages (mutual illusion tools) can easily be in full cooperation with the oneness of nature when we know oneness is real and separate parts are an illusion.

It is this mutually created illusion tool called "separate parts" or "human language" that allows the universe to be self-conscious, to know what it is doing while it is doing it. While fully and simultaneously doing both, when we have mastered the full skill of self-consciousness the cooperation between the two always gives priority to the oneness of nature (reality) and second priority to the mutually created illusion of separate parts (illusion) that has allowed the universe to mature to where it can be self-conscious in billions of locations at the same time through us.

Thinking Pain

Here is another thing to note: we only begin to search for the next layer of maturity when we discover we are experiencing what I call "thinking pain." This is when we notice that we are still not *naturally and effortlessly* happy as we move through our days. It is this that reveals to us that there must be something more to learn we do not know about the skill of self-consciousness.

If we are aware there are layers of maturity of the skill of self-consciousness, we will search to relieve this thinking pain by identifying the next layer of maturity of this skill. If we are not aware they exist, we will search many other places for relief and often go in circles. However we will not find some significant and consistent relief from it until we discover and master the smaller skill of the next layer of the total skill of self-consciousness.

This is the only thing that *reduces* thinking pain. And achieving full maturity in the skill of self-consciousness is the only thing that *ends* it and replaces it with the consistent experience of the *natural and effortless fundamental feeling of happiness, or inner peace,* as the container within which everything else is experienced as secondary in importance.

In our thinking at the Elder Layer, the *accurate fundamental inside belief* becomes the container within which we experience everything else as secondary in importance, equally valuable but secondary in importance.

Since Two Years Old We Have Also Been Using the Oneness Pattern of Thinking

The most interesting thing we discover at the Elder Layer is that we have been using the priority pattern of thinking since we learned a language.

We realize that if oneness is a fact, not just an idea, then we must have also been using the oneness pattern of thinking since we were two years old. Oneness is always present and can't be escaped. So, without knowing it, simultaneously and unconsciously we must have been using the oneness pattern of thinking while we were using our separate parts pattern of thinking as if it is the only pattern of thinking possible.

The oneness pattern of thinking we have been using since using the separate parts pattern of thinking is choosing where to focus our attention.

There are an immense number of places and activities upon which we could choose to focus our attention. Relative to all the others the one we are choosing each moment is the one we are choosing to give *priority*. This activity, the choice of where to focus our attention, is using the priority pattern of thinking, the oneness pattern of thinking.

We can't do anything in time and space until we choose where to focus our attention, until we have used the oneness pattern of thinking. Oneness cannot be escaped.

So we realize we have been using both patterns of thinking all along and we have always given priority to the priority pattern of thinking, to the oneness pattern of thinking, even when we were acting as if we were only giving priority to the separate parts pattern of thinking.

This is why wise leaders have been able to lead us into working well together by knowing that they simply have to change our pattern of thinking to the oneness pattern. When a meeting is polarized, one group thinking we should do blue and another thinking we should do red, they simply ask, "What is the priority here? What is best for the good of all?" Without being aware that everyone's fundamental pattern of thinking has been changed into the oneness pattern, all begin to give priority to putting the parts together to make a whole and the competitive football game between the blue team and the red team disappears.

Here is the story of how I discovered this skill.

In 2000 I was the leader of a team trying to buy Ben & Jerry's. A time came, at 2 am in the morning, when negotiations broke down. The twenty or so representatives of Unilever, that was to become our minority partner and provide the distribution through the warehouse system that was essential, their investment bankers from Goldman Sachs, and their lawyers from Skadden Arps had gotten up from the boardroom table, gathered their winter coats and briefcases, and were leaving through the boardroom door. I had used all of my facilitation skills to try to keep negotiations proceeding and they had not worked. I knew I could not let them leave the room. My leverage to get them back to the negotiating table would be greatly reduced.

In desperation, I pulled something out of my back pocket. It was all I could think of that might work.

When half of them were already outside the boardroom door, I asked all to come back into the room with a voice that suggested I had something new to put on the table. They froze where they were. They looked at each other to determine what to do. They non-verbally reached agreement to return to the table. They put their coats and briefcases down somewhere and sat at the table, spiritually or actually with their hands folded on the table in front of them, and looked at me as if to say, "You better have something damn good to say!"

When all were fully settled back in their chairs at the large wood boardroom table I spoke, "I would like to ask everyone to be silent for a few moments. While you are silent think about the answer to these two questions: What is the priority here? What is best for the good of all?"

I then went into total silence myself and very self-consciously looked at the table so I would not meet anyone's eyes.

We were probably only silent for two or three minutes but to them it probably felt like ten minutes. I am quite sure they had probably never experienced anything like this in negotiations to buy a company on the 57th floor of a building on Wall Street.

I eventually looked up and the lead negotiator for Goldman Sachs caught my eye and motioned with them a request to speak. I motioned back that that would be fine.

He presented their position in a way that fully accommodated our position. Jim Steiker, my lead negotiator, responded by restating our position in a way that fully accommodated their position. We were back into negotiations as if no polarization had ever happened.

Twice over the next couple of months we ended up in an almost deal breaking polarization and both times I did the same thing using the same words and we were back into negotiations within minutes as if the polarization had not occurred.

It was only weeks afterwards that I was able to figure out why this worked. By switching the pattern of thinking from polarization to prioritization I had switched their pattern of thinking from separate parts to oneness.

The natural result was that they began putting the parts together to make a whole, the opposite of blue verses red.

It was this experience that had me discover the importance of not only changing our belief to the accurate one and our self-definition to the accurate one, but also changing the self-conscious primary pattern of our thinking, the wordrack upon which we hang our thoughts, to the oneness pattern of thinking.

It is giving priority to priorities.

They were not even aware that I had changed their pattern of thinking by the way I asked those two questions. At the time I was not aware it had occurred either. Out of desperation I had bungled into doing it and only later discovered why it worked.

All three changes are essential to master the Elder Layer of maturity in the skill of self-consciousness.

The Material Now and the Eternal Now

We also become aware that there are really two "nows," which I have labeled the "material now" and the "eternal now."

In our thinking the *material now* is operating on the separate parts assumption. It experiences the past, present, and future as three separate things. The *eternal now* is the experience of the past, present, and future as one experience. As we come to understand this, while fully aware of both, we always give priority in our thinking to the eternal now over the material now.

Fundamentally, language is the creation of a polarity, hot—cold, and then the degrees of differences between them: boiling—hot—warm—room temperature—chilly—cold—freezing. Therefore, to represent oneness in language we always have to represent two things, the two ends of a polarity in language. So the *eternal now* is how we represent oneness in the *time* concept in language, as all the past, present, and future as one experience. Defining ourselves as first the entire universe and secondly our physical bodies is how we represent oneness in the language concept of *space*. Time and space are the most fundamental opposites in language that represent separate parts.

Here is how I practically use this knowledge. At times of discomfort with what is going on I will remember there is no past or future, really, just priorities in the eternal now. This has me instantly turn my attention to the priority in the moment. It then always becomes obvious: whatever is best for the common good. I was always unconsciously giving priority to something else.

Relative Experience of Oneness with Another

Finally, we are able to sit with another, look him or her in the eyes, and settle into a mutual safe and receptive experience of love, *of the mutual relative self-conscious feeling of oneness.* (It is the same way we behave when eyes to eyes with a baby. We become *unilaterally fully receptive as if there is no second thing to fear* only now we are doing this with another self-conscious adult.)

This feeling, the relative feeling of oneness, is the only relative feeling that does not have degrees of feeling it.

Every other relative feeling does have degrees. If we are close friends, on a scale of one to ten with ten being the closest, the feeling of friendship could be at a ten. If we have not seen each other for many years, it may be experienced as at a seven or six. There are degrees of the experience of all other relative feelings.

However there are not degrees of difference when experiencing the relative feeling of oneness. It is the only relative feeling that does not have degrees of experiencing it. Thus we cannot get better or worse at it. We can only be aware of feeling it or not feeling it. It is a local experience of the fundamental feeling of happiness, the feeling of it where our attention is focused.

Thus all we can do is hang out in it as the mutually chosen container within which we do everything else, everything in time and space, as a secondary activity.

This is also the experience of what we have labeled "true love," love between any two people: lovers, parent–child, siblings, friends, workmates, whomever. It is the experience of the oneness of nature mutually chosen and self-consciously known as a relative feeling, a feeling between two of us, or a group of us, when our attention is focused on our relationship with each other.

This is the relative feeling of oneness, the local feeling of oneness, because we are only experiencing it where our attention is focused.

Once we have mastered the first six layers of the skill of self-consciousness as habits we can then sit with another or a group who also understands this and settle into the mutual feeling of the oneness of nature, of love. *This is the only relative feeling that does not have degrees of feeling it.* Therefore we can't get better or worse at it. All we can do is hang out in it as a self-consciously known feeling and do other things in time and space together, *now always as secondary in importance.* This is a fun self-conscious place to be with another. My friends and I call it "the love place." Knowing this becomes a knowledge skill.

It is particularly important for romantic lovers, our most intimate relationship, to know this as a joint self-conscious experience. If this is known as a *mutually known skill,* when discomfort or conflict emerges we can freely choose to come back to it as the *container feeling* within which we experience everything else as secondary in importance.

It is at the sixth layer, the Elder Layer, where we know that, fundamentally, there are only two things, oneness and human languages. Both are equally valuable and we have found the mature relationship of priorities between the two.

Summary of Skills to Learn at the Elder Layer

Thus, in summary, at the Elder Layer there is much new knowledge and many habits to be changed. Here is a summary of the main ones described in this section:

1. We discover the accurate fundamental belief in words, that the universe is an indivisible whole.

2. We now know there is not a second thing to receive our power. Therefore, it is necessary to give priority to discovering the accurate fundamental belief in our direct experience. Then we can at anytime turn our attention there and confirm we are accurate. This way we have kept our power and achieved full freedom. Doing this is being a personal scientist. It is necessary to master the skill of being a personal scientist to discover the next and final layer of maturity of the skill of self-consciousness.

3. We choose the accurate self-definition "I am the universe that will not

die and secondly my physical body that will die."

4. We choose to give priority to the oneness pattern of thinking (giving priority to priorities) and second priority to the separate parts pattern of thinking (choosing between this or that in time and space) while fully doing both.

5. We recognize that we are now aware of two kinds of beliefs, outside and inside beliefs. Outside beliefs are the beliefs we have been choosing as our fundamental belief up to now. We give our power to them and obey them. Inside beliefs are the result of turning our attention to our immediate direct experience to discover the accurate fundamental belief. We describe it in words so we can talk about it with others and ourselves. However this is secondary in importance to keeping our power, all of it.

6. Studying our direct experience to identify our freely chosen fundamental belief is the only action that ends partial freedom in the belief that it is full freedom.

7. Human language is a mutual illusion tool we have created that allows us to be self-conscious. That is the sole purpose of this tool. Its necessary assumption that the universe is an immense number of separate parts is not accurate. However it is this mutually created tool that allows the universe through us to be self-conscious at billions of locations at the same time. Therefore it is as valuable as being aware of the oneness of nature. Since it is an illusion it can be given second priority to our direct experience of the oneness of nature and be in full and effortless cooperation with it. Illusions are never a threat to reality.

8. The assumption at the Adult Layer that we are our physical bodies is a good thing. It is part of the process of mastering that layer of maturity in the skill of self-consciousness. It is not possible to master the Elder Layer without having first thought things through and chosen a fundamental belief within the assumption that separate parts are real (Adult Layer). Without this action we would not eventually seek to find the accurate fundamental belief.

9. Thinking pain is a gift. It reveals there is another layer of maturity of the skill of self-consciousness to discover.

10. We also recognize there are two "nows," the material now and the eternal now. The material now is the now between the past and the future,

perceived as three separate parts. The eternal now is all the past, present, and future as one experience. We now always give priority to living within the eternal now and second priority to simultaneously living in the material now. This has us naturally and effortlessly give priority to priorities with the highest priority being whatever we determine to be best for the common good of us all.

11. Since two years old, when we began to use a human language, we have been using the oneness pattern of thinking as well as the separate parts pattern of thinking. Where we choose to focus our attention is giving it priority over all the other possible places we could choose to focus it. We can't do anything in time and space without first choosing where to focus our attention. The latter is giving priority to the use of the oneness pattern of thinking. And,

12. It is possible to come to know with another in direct experience the relative feeling of oneness, the self-conscious experience of oneness in a particular relationship, what we will call "local oneness." Unlike all other relative feelings where there are degrees of feeling them, here there are no degrees of the relative feeling of oneness. Therefore, we can't get better or worse at it. We can only hang out in it as the container when doing anything else in time and space.

MATURE ELDER

Like the initial experience of our discovery of each layer, many of us think we have achieved the highest layer of maturity when we have mastered the Elder Layer. However we have not.

Our daily experience is still not the consistent and easy joy of happiness we have intuitively known is possible since the Toddler Layer. We are still experiencing some thinking pain, some absence of full contentment. By this time we know what this means. It means there must be the smaller skill of another layer of the skill of self-consciousness to discover and master. So we set out to find it.

We discover it when we ask ourselves the following questions, "What is the experience of being the universe? If the universe is an indivisible whole and we, therefore, are first the universe, *what is the "direct experience" of being the universe?"*

This is different than going to our direct experience to identify the accurate fundamental belief. This is a search to identify the direct experience of being the universe.

By mutual choice we now know how to experience the joy of happiness as a relative feeling with another (local oneness), but how do we know this joy at all times wherever we are and regardless of what is going on? If I am first the universe, what is the *experience* of being the universe?

Let's try a few small experiments. With each one going forward take as much time as you want.

First, take a few moments looking up from reading to focus your attention on this statement by saying it a few times to yourself: "I am my physical body." You know you are your physical body; so this will not be hard to turn your attention to this fact. What is important is to be very aware of giving priority with your *attention* to being your physical body.

So take a few moments to do this before turning to the next page.

By saying the words a few times focus your attention on the fact this is true: "I am my physical body".

If you study what happened closely, you will probably notice that you were giving priority to the words "I am my physical body," not the *experience* of being it, or at least going back and forth between the two.

We have been living within the world of words since we learned a language. We will continue to do so unless we learn how to *choose* to give priority to *experience* instead of words. So lets learn to do that now.

This time again give primary attention to saying "I am my physical body" to yourself again and be fully comfortable that you are primarily giving attention to the words. Then change to have your attention give priority to the experience of being your physical body. We are most familiar with doing this when we are sick. Then we give priority with our attention to the experience of what is going on in our body. So this also is not hard to do.

What we want to accomplish here is to know the difference between giving priority with our attention to the **words** *or the* **experience.**

By the way, the priority of our attention is always switching from one thing to another. It is studying our environment to make sure we are safe and taking advantage of opportunities to mature. So, do not be disturbed if your attention leaves where you have chosen to focus it; this is normal. Just choose again to focus it where you want to focus it.

So lets give this a try. Again turn the priority of your attention to the *words* "I am my physical body" by saying them to yourself a few times. Then switch the priority of your attention to the *experience* of being your physical body *and be sure to notice the difference when you do it.*

Then turn to the next page.

First say "I am my physical body" a few times focusing on the *words*. Then choose to switch to have the priority of your attention be on the *experience* of being your physical body and notice the *difference*.

My guess is that when you turned your attention to the *experience of being your physical body* there was the experience of being alive, with sensations, feelings, and thought. You primarily experienced "self" as a seeing, hearing, smelling, tactile and tasting experience. When focused on the words, this was absent. If you take a moment now and again focus your attention on the words "I am my physical body" you clearly notice they are not alive. Whatever is your experience when focused on *the words* it is not the experience of being alive. They are mutually agreed upon illusions, words. *The opposite of being alive.*

It is essential that we come to know the difference between having the priority of our attention on words or experience.

Whenever we are being self-conscious words are always between us and what we are experiencing. They are what allow us to be self-conscious. Therefore we are always giving priority to one of the two of them; so it is important that we know the difference and able to choose to give priority to either.

The reason this is important is because the only way we can escape giving our power to a second thing that does not exist is to know how to give priority to our immediate and direct experience. Only then have we kept our power, used it to determine from a study of our direct experience that the universe is an indivisible whole, and are then able to easily and effortlessly live this truth in our behavior.

Now that we *know* that the universe is an indivisible whole primarily from a study of our immediate and direct experience *we can turn our attention to the experience of it.* Remember, the size of the universe is not what is most important. It is our relationship to the rest of the parts of it that is most important. We now know in direct experience from keeping our power and studying our breathing that it is an indivisible whole. Now we want to learn to focus our attention on *the experience of it being the indivisible universe.*

This time you might like to have your eyes closed but you do not have to. This time turn your attention to saying the words "I am the experience of being the universe" a few times knowing you are primarily focusing on the words. Then switch to have your attention be on the *experience* of this fact.

Then turn to the next page.

First, by saying it a few times to yourself, focus your attention on the *words* "I am the experience of being the universe" perhaps with your eyes closed. Then choose to switch to have your attention on the *experience* of it. Then take notice of the *difference* between the two.

You probably eventually noticed a sense of calm, of inner peace. If so it is obvious why you did: if you are the universe there is no second thing that could be in conflict with you. As a result the experience was *inner peace, the absence of the possibility of conflict.*

Be comfortable doing the above exercise again, many times. The experience of inner peace (the fundamental feeling of happiness) is different from all relative experiences. Our experience of our physical bodies in relationship to any other part of the universe gives us sensual, feeling, and opinion experiences. There are none of those relative experiences when experiencing inner peace. It is the absence of any of them. It is not the experience of relating with a second thing. Thus the only way we can know we are experiencing it is when we have the experience of inner peace.

The experience of inner peace is how we know our attention is on the experience of being the universe. It is the only evidence of it. It is the experience of being all things without the possibility of conflict (the fundamental feeling of happiness only now with the mature skill of self-consciousness fully present).

Once you know the experience of inner peace from doing the above exercise you can learn to choose it directly. It is no longer necessary to walk through this exercise to choose it as a direct experience. You will then choose to have it be your primary direct experience at all times and to have anything else be secondary in importance. *This is living in reality first and in the activity of words second.* This is the experience of enlightenment, the state of grace, and full human maturity as a skill.

We now *primarily* experience the universe the way we primarily experience our physical bodies: *as an experience.* As a sensual, feeling, and thinking experience. For each of us, the universe is now our whole physical body. We just only have sole and compete inside control over each of our particular physical body parts of it.

Mastery of this skill is the mastery of the Mature Elder Layer of maturity, the highest layer of maturity of the skill of self-consciousness.

Now you can realize that everything is really happening inside you, inside whom you actually are. Anyone who assumes conflict is real is operating at one of the lower layers of maturity in the skill of self-consciousness. A mature elder understands this and responds with compassion. He or she knows that it was not possible to have reached the Mature Elder Layer of maturity without at one time also assuming each of the lower layers of maturity was the highest layer. So compassion is natural and effortless. His or her attention, therefore, turns to identifying the best unique action of love that is participation in the maturation of the universe.

In our current capitalist economy it would be to invite all competitors to join in voluntary agreements (they all need to keep their power) that give priority to the common good and second priority to competition while fully doing both. This choice of priorities honors their right of free choice and their responsibility to keep their power while also honoring that of others who may later want to enter that particular market. It is voluntary collective action that honors the reality that the universe is an indivisible whole and, therefore, we want to always work directly with others to give priority to the common good, to our mutual maturation.

Let yourself do the above three exercises as often as you like until you are able to easily choose to focus your attention on the words, the experience of being your physical body, and the experience of being the universe. You will naturally gravitate toward giving priority at all times to the latter as the container within which you experience everything else. It is the most enjoyable container. In my judgement the goal of all forms of meditation and prayer are to have one be able to turn one's attention by choice to these three places and ultimately learn to always give priority to the experience of the oneness of nature (Mature Elder Layer).

When I find myself relating very separate from another, one of the techniques I use to take myself into this experience with the other person is to reframe what is occurring in my thinking. I learned this with my ten-year-old daughter when we were at the beach last summer. I realized I was acting very separate from her. When I did what I will describe below she immediately began looking me comfortably and steadily in the eyes as we talked, affirming a deeper level of intimacy between us. Being ten years old she naturally went where there was greater comfort. However, I have found that it works well with adults as well.

I choose to experience the other person and me as inside something and relating as two parts of a whole, as if we are two thinking abilities talking to ourself. This immediately has the tension evaporate and replaced with the experience of inner peace. It becomes the container of what is occurring and I am able to manage it from that experiential place.

What is also remarkable is that it almost always instantly changes the behavior of the other to begin to join me there. It is obviously a more enjoyable experience to which the other person now has access in our relationship. So the other naturally and effortlessly gravitates toward joining me there, as my daughter fully and immediately did. What is also remarkable is that I ask nothing of the other person. I only changed the framework of my thinking and experience.

To summarize this presentation on the layers of maturity of the skill of self-consciousness, when we are learning a language our priority is the recognition of differences. Then it becomes the mastery of the skill of self-consciousness that allows us to choose among the differences. Until we discover its existence in direct experience, awareness of the oneness of nature is a mystery. When we do become aware of it in direct experience, we naturally and effortlessly integrate it into our behavior each moment.

Then we do a reversal of the priorities of the three dimensions of the skill of self-consciousness. Now at all times *the oneness of nature* is our priority, using the *skill of self-consciousness* is our second priority, and the *recognition of differences* is our third priority.

Now let's figure out how to *represent in language* the experience of being the universe.

Allow me to give you a hint: to represent it in a human language it has to have two parts, the two ends of a polarity. If you feel like it, before reading further see what you come up with as the two ends *that represent in a human language* the direct experience of being the universe. What is your guess?

We now know that when we are being self-conscious our human language always exists between what we are thinking or perceiving and us. We also know that to represent oneness in language we need to describe it in two ways. As mentioned earlier, the fundamental structure of language is polarization, the making up of opposites: up-down, right-left, high-low. Thus, *in language* there is both a *personal experience* (inner experience) and *social experience* (relationship with the other parts of the universe) of being the universe. These are the two most fundamental opposites *represented in language* of the experience of being the universe.

The Personal Experience of Being the Universe

Let's first describe the *personal experience of being the universe.*

There is nowhere for the universe to go to or from where it is not already. Therefore, the only thing a self-conscious universe can do is watch what is going on.

The personal experience of being the universe is the experience of primarily being the watcher, not "a watcher" but "the watcher."

And what is it watching? If maturation is the fundamental process in nature and it is always naturally and effortlessly occurring, *then the universe is primarily watching this maturation process.* It is the only place where there is activity, something to watch as it is changing.

We discover there is nothing more personally enjoyable than watching and experiencing the natural and effortless process of the maturation of the universe because it can always be witnessed and experienced as occurring.

For instance, we now know that each person is always giving priority to one of the layers of maturity in the skill of self-consciousness. We also know that if they knew of the next higher layer they would naturally and effortlessly be fully embracing it. We also know they can't skip layers. About this they do not have choice. This is nature. So compassion, the feeling of moving as one with another in understanding, and forgiveness if necessary, is always the primary feeling that emerges when witnessing another operating at a lower layer of maturity. And it is experienced as a "one-with experience," not as a "superior experience." This sustains the joy of happiness as the container of everything we witness. It is experienced as another part of *our* maturation.

In any moment the direct personal experience of being the universe is giving priority wherever we are focusing our attention to the joy of watching the fundamental process of maturation that is always occurring.

It is similar to the relationship between a parent and a small child. The parent is at all times watching to be sure the child is safe and experiencing opportunities to mature, what we can label "local maturation watching." The difference is that now we are the universe watching ourselves, the universe, from the particular place we are standing to be sure all the parts with which we are able to relate are safe and experiencing opportunities to mature.

We now understand the mature relationship between our human languages (the mutual illusion tool) and the oneness of nature (reality) and how to prioritize them in the patterns of our thinking. That is, we have mastered the skill at the Elder Layer and have turned it into a habit. *Therefore we are no longer trying to further unravel the riddle of the relationship between oneness and language.* Our attention can now be focused on mastering this next, and last, smaller skill of the total basic skill of self-consciousness.

And, as the universe, we know there is no place we are going to or from where we are not already. We also know there is not a second thing to fear. So the only thing to do is to enjoy being a watcher of the universe's beautiful process of maturation. Just as we enjoy watching for safety and directly participating in a child's fundamental process of maturation, now wherever we are standing we always primarily enjoy watching to ensure safety, and as we will see below, to then directly participate in the universe's fundamental process of maturation.

Full personal maturity in the skill of self-consciousness is when nothing is distracting us from giving priority each moment to direct self-conscious participation in the maturation of the universe. The smaller skills of the layers of maturity of the skill of self-consciousness have been turned into habits and we also habitually know their priority relationship to each other.

On the inside this frees us to primarily enjoy the experience of self-consciously participating in maturation without distractions.

We also soon notice that most of the involuntary thoughts that come into our thinking are about our physical body and its relationship with other parts of the universe. When we witness this we realize it is the result of the habit up to now of primarily identifying with our physical body as who we primarily are. As a result we then decide we want to figure out how we can instead have our primary involuntary thoughts be on how in the present moment we can directly participate in the maturation of the universe.

We eventually discover that the only way to accomplish this is to change our self-definition. What we choose as our self-definition determines how we naturally and effortlessly behave. If it is the most mature self-definition, that "I am first the universe that does not die and secondly my physical body that will die," our primary involuntary thoughts will begin to reflect this self-definition. They will then primarily be on our enjoyment of having achieved full maturity in the skill of self-consciousness and how we can best participate in the maturation process of nature. This takes us to the other side of the polarity of how in language we describe the experience of the oneness of nature.

Finally, we become aware that we are always having two self-conscious experiences: the universe being self-conscious through us and our physical bodies being self-conscious through the use of a human language. I have labeled the first "knowing mind" and the second "rational thinking."

If the universe is an indivisible whole there is only one mind we are all using and billions of self-conscious human thinkers. We are each primarily using the one mind and secondly have our collection of experiences and memories.

Rational thinking is always using words as an intermediary. It exists in words and we reach conclusions in words. It is always unconsciously or self-consciously in the mutually agreed upon illusion tool of separate parts.

Knowing mind does not use a human language as an intermediary. It is direct knowing. You are at all times using this skill. For instance, right now you know where you are in the room and where you are not. You know your name, the particular clothes you are wearing, and how your bottom is feeling on the chair. You know you have agreed to meet someone at a particular time tomorrow. Knowing mind is knowing things without having to organize words into rational lines.

However there is more possible with knowing mind if you are open to experiencing it.

Knowing mind is the universe living self-consciously in and through each of us. It has access to all information and is constantly downloading into our senses, feelings, and thoughts valuable information for us in our particular situation. This information is always in alignment with the maturation of the universe, the common good. We can learn to be self-consciously open to it.

There is one indicator we can observe that reveals knowing mind is naturally and effortlessly always giving priority to maturation through us. When we are in the shower or waking up in the morning and the thoughts that pop into our thinking are the exact thoughts we need: where we left our automobile keys, the particular piece we forgot to include in the report we wrote, or the important piece of information we failed to share with someone the day before. This is the evidence we can witness of knowing mind assisting us in our maturation. Of all the thoughts the universe could bring into our thinking, it brings the exact important pieces of information we need. We can discover that it is always doing it, make words secondary in importance, and listen for it each moment.

There are two ways we can double check to be sure information is from knowing mind: it comes directly from experience—the universe—and it is information fully in alignment with the fundamental process of maturation within the oneness of nature. Some people call this "intuition." Mahatma Gandhi and others have called it the "little voice within." Now that you are or are becoming a fully free human being you can choose to be open to this constant stream of information and become aware of its consistent wisdom.

Secondly, during my life I have gone on many long fasts of only water. The first thing my physical body jettisons is rational thinking. It is not necessary. Knowing mind can handle everything. Thus throughout history people have used fasting as a way to become familiar with the direct experience of being open to knowing mind so they can master the skill of consistently listening to it with rational thinking also being present.

While always comfortable using both skills of self-consciousness, Mature Elders always give priority to knowing mind over rational thinking because it sustains the experience of inner peace. *It is giving priority to the direct self-conscious experience of being the universe.*

I have had many direct knowing mind experiences, but one was quite dramatic.

One dark evening, as I was leaving my daughter's home and walking the ten car lengths to my car, this question came into my thinking: "What would I do if a car coming from the other direction came fully into my lane and continued to come towards me?" This had never happened to me and this question had never come into my thinking before, but my thinking began to answer the question: "I would have to quickly judge if it was going to continue or head back into its lane. If I judged it was going to continue, I would have to drive left into its lane. If I judged it was going to eventually try to go back into its lane, I would have to drive off the road to the right. In either case it would be very important that I maintain control of the car the entire time."

In less than ten minutes this happened. I determined the other car would try to go back into its lane so I drove off the road to the right, down into and up out of a small ditch, and drove the car at a near 45 degree angle along a grass and rock hill until I could get back down into and out of the ditch and back onto the highway. The entire time I was watchful to make sure I maintained control of the car.

Knowing mind fully lived it in my thinking before it happened. Knowing mind has full access to all information regardless of the mutually agreed upon illusions of separate parts (time and space). We want to learn to always be available to its information downloads.

The Social Experience of Being the Universe

Now let's describe the *social experience of being the universe*. It is the answer to the question, "What is the priority in our activities with others?"

Each moment the priority in our activities is whatever we each judge to be the best unique thing we can do with our physical bodies that is in direct participation with the fundamental process of maturation.

It is *unique* because no one else is ever standing where we are each standing. Secondly, each moment there are many activities we can choose to do that participate in the maturation of the universe. Since it is the fundamental process of nature, each moment we always want to choose the best action we are capable of taking so we are in the fullest process possible of participation in maturation.

One moment it could be helping a child learn to walk, the next moment it could be picking up the paper towels that missed the trash can in the public bathroom, and the next moment it could be facilitating peace among some nations. No one else is ever standing where each of us is standing. Therefore each moment it is always what we each judge to be the *best unique thing* we can do that is participation in the maturation of the universe, the one indivisible whole.

In language we have now identified the second half of the experience of enlightenment, the state of grace, or full maturity in the skill of self-consciousness. We have identified the *social experience* of it.

As a result, we now know what to do each moment. Life is now experienced as meaningful.

Eventually these two ways of representing in language the experience of being the universe, the personal and social ways, merge into one habitual experience. But we will now be able to fully take it apart and represent what is going on in our human language so we can talk about it with others and ourselves, particularly for the purpose of assisting others to understand it.

Our personal-social experience becomes self-consciously moving as one with the indivisible universe by primarily watching the fundamental process of maturation in nature and actively participating by each moment doing what we each judge to be the best unique action we can execute as self-conscious participants in it.

Herein this is labeled "eldering," a word that has not existed in the English language until now. Yet it has been known and lived by many throughout history. And with good eldering by our parents and others in our communities, we can each master all the smaller skills of the total skill of self-consciousness in their natural progression by the time we are in our twenties. We will then, from that point forward, give priority to the joy of eldering.

This, we discover, allows us to know by free choice and skill the consistent joy of the fundamental feeling of happiness. All thinking pain is now usually gone, it does not easily return, and we know it will never permanently return. We have now mastered the skill of always being able to return to it. We will at times forget and regress into behaving as if a lower layer of maturity is the highest layer, and then thinking pain will again be experienced.

We now love thinking pain! And we realize we should have loved it all along!

It is what has guided us up the layers of maturity of the skill of self-consciousness and is now sustaining us at being able to continue operating, or return to operating, at the highest layer.

We now know how to sustain joy and that we can return to it by free choice in any moment. It feels like driving down an unlit road on a moonless night when both of our headlights have burnt out. It is almost going into the ditch on each side that reveals the direction of the middle of the road. If we lose our way it is thinking pain that reveals to us the correct direction to the discovery of the fundamental feeling of the joy of happiness.

It is also now much easier to identify the unconscious habits we chose to survive during childhood that are still disrupting our relations with others. Psychotherapists will now focus on assisting their clients to first master the smaller skills of each of the layers of maturity of the skill of self-consciousness in the natural progression before giving primary focus to identifying and ending immature and disruptive unconscious habits. Without knowing in direct experience the mature habit to replace the immature habit it is very difficult to end the immature habit. And without knowing of the existence and importance of eldering ourselves up the layers of maturity, we can go in circles at our current layer. We need to be focused on the habit we want, not on the one we do not want. The nurturing of any behavior is the result of focusing our attention on it. Therefore, the primary responsibility of psychotherapists is to elder their clients into full maturity in the skill of self-consciousness.

The Three Dimensions of the Skill of Self-Consciousness

Now lets take a look at the relationship between the layers of maturity and the three dimensions of the skill of self-consciousness.

As described earlier, I now know there are three dimensions of self-consciousness. I have named them the *recognition of differences,* the creation of the *mutual illusion tool of separate parts (time and space) that allows us to be self-conscious,* and *the self-conscious experience of the oneness of nature.*

We become aware of sensations at the Baby Layer. We become aware of differences, as well as the fundamental feeling of happy-not-happy, at the Toddler Layer. We master the human illusion tool of separate parts (time and space) that allows us to create and use a language and thereby become self-conscious during the Child to Elder Layers. We only master the third dimension of giving priority to the experience of being the universe at the

THE RELATIONSHIP BETWEEN THE LAYERS OF MATURITY AND THREE DIMENSIONS OF THE HUMAN SKILL OF SELF-CONSCIOUSNESS

Mature Elder	Priority is the self-conscious experience of the oneness of nature: Eldering	*Mastery of the Self-Conscious Experience of the Oneness of Nature*
Elder	Priority is the accurate fundamental belief that the universe is an indivisible whole: personal science	*Mastery of the Skill of Self-Consciousness*
Adult	Priority is fundamental belief	" "
Teen	Priority is free choice	" "
Child	Priority is wants and relative feelings	" "
Toddler	Priority is fundamental feeling (happy-not happy)	*Recognition of Differences*
Baby	Priority is sensations	" "

Mature Elder Layer, the full mastery of the skill of self-consciousness.

As I have stated earlier, I believe that we, as a human species, are currently going through the process of mastering the Elder Layer of the skill of self-consciousness. Some of us, in fact more and more of us each day, are mastering the skill of the Mature Elder Layer. It is giving priority to the *self-conscious experience of the oneness of nature*. The very practical result is that the priority in our activity each moment is to execute the best unique action for maturing our global self-conscious consensus agreements based on facts. As a result we will be consistently reorganizing our lives with each other to give this priority.

The best words I have found to state this most fundamental belief at the Elder Layer are, "the universe is an indivisible whole." You may choose other words, such as "oneness," or "unity." What is important is that they accurately represent the fundamental fact that *the universe operates as an indivisible whole.*

Super Beliefs

We can still choose what can be called "super beliefs," additional beliefs that are on top of and given priority that are not part of the *skill* of self-consciousness. We may have religious beliefs, usually assuming the existence of a God, heaven, and hell where each is separate from the universe. Like some scientists today, we could believe in parallel universes. We could believe that we had past lives as other people. We could believe that our ancestors are still fully present and able to communicate with us. We can hold any super beliefs we choose.

The focus in this book is on what can be directly experienced as layers of maturity of the skill of self-consciousness.

Self-consciousness is a skill, not a belief. Any super belief can at any time be placed on top of it and given priority.

So the mastery of the skill of self-consciousness in no way limits anyone's ability to give priority to a super belief.

Projection Protection

We always project our way of being in the world onto others and assume they will behave as we would behave. In psychology this is called "projection." Particularly when one has mastered the last two layers, this can be dangerous.

If one is not prepared one will assume another will behave as we would behave. If they don't, we could get very hurt and angry. This is especially true if it is someone with whom we have a very close relationship where our investment in the relationship is very high.

I have learned to provide myself some protection against accidentally doing this. The phrase I remind myself of a few times each day as protection against making this mistake may not work for you but it works for me, and that is all that matters. The phrase I use is "Everyone is crazy and so am I."

This is my way of making sure I am not surprised when another or I behave in a very immature way. This triggers me into compassion and forgiveness instead of hurt and anger.

No matter how good we have gotten at the skill of self-consciousness, we will all have moments of regression to giving priority to one of the lower layers of maturity. Having a little Projection Protection active inside us daily can have us more easily experience compassion toward others and ourselves in these moments.

Affirmation Creating

If you are like me you often like to create an affirmation (or *mantra*) to use during the day to remind you to behave the way you would like to behave when out and about in the world. I find that I usually have one that emerges in my meditation time.

First I would like to suggest that you always create your own and change them from time to time as you judge wise. This is part of keeping your power rather than giving it to another.

I came up with one this morning I liked: "I am the universe extending love." Then as I was later driving out of the driveway and using it as a reminder of who I primarily am, I realized I was using the time-space thinking structure, extending love from one place to another. This error, I realized, could have me feel upset when another to whom I am extending love does not respond in kind...that projection problem.

So I then restructured the affirmation to be sure it was using the oneness thinking structure: "I am the universe participating in love."

I share this because language is always between whatever we are thinking or perceiving and us. Therefore it is important for us to learn to always use the priority pattern of thinking that represents oneness as real and separate parts as secondary in importance. The better we get at this the less the possibility of accidentally disrupting our relationships with others and ourselves.

It is Essential to Realize that a Higher Layer of Maturity in the Skill of Self-Consciousness is not Possible

The consistent experience of the fundamental feeling of the joy of happiness as the container of all that is occurring reveals that a higher layer of maturity in the skill of self-consciousness is not possible.

What could be greater than defining "self" as "all that exists"? All time, all space, and all that exists? A larger self-definition is not possible. And what could be more enjoyable than knowing how to self-consciously sustain living each moment in this most fundamental truth? And the fact that the joy is consistent and without disruption, except, of course, when we forget, reveals that a higher layer of personal maturation in the skill of self-consciousness is not possible. Thus, it becomes clear that this is the *highest possible layer* of human maturity in the basic skill of self-consciousness.

It is essential to recognize this.

Only then will we choose to give priority to eldering, to the maturation of our true self, the indivisible universe, instead of only the maturation in the skill of self-consciousness in our physical body, a part of the universe. The giving of *priority* to our personal maturation is over. From this point on our highest priority is the maturation of our total self, the universe.

Our highest priority is now the enjoyment of eldering. Achieving full maturity in the skill of self-consciousness is just the beginning of a human life. From then on our priority is eldering.

Mahatma Gandhi's Genius

By the way, the genius of Mahatma Gandhi was that he understood that the universe is an indivisible whole. He then came up with a method of social maturation based on it. He created a new word in Hindi to name it: *satyagraha*. The definition he gave it was "the natural force of truth." Another translation could be "the natural force of the oneness of nature."

The essence of it is to always *primarily* relate with the primary good intention in another. He knew that by *the nature of the universe being an indivisible whole* the other's highest priority is always the common good of us all. About that they do not have choice.

This is why when he was unable using persuasion to get those in power to change a social injustice, he chose to not cooperate with it to force them to think more deeply about it. He also always announced significantly in advance what his non-cooperation activity would be. He hoped that to avoid having to deal with it they would change (mature) their thinking and it would not be necessary.

His goal was not to just change their thinking. His goal was to change the thinking of all involved. It was to mature our consensus of what are the more mature agreements and behaviors now possible for us.

The more mature social agreement for which he is best known was having England *and the Indian people* realize it was time to allow the Indian people to have their independence. Most in both countries eventually agreed with him and England gave India its independence.

Sadly this very mature strategy for bringing about maturation in the way we all think became named in English "non-violence". *In reality* "the natural force of truth" does not have an opposite: there is not a natural force of non-truth. *In language* non-violence does have an opposite: violence. The result is that many think Gandhi's method was using non-violence rather than violence. They forget that a couple of times he supported Prime

Minister Jawaharlal Nehru using the army.

Violence may be necessary, but only as a last resort. If someone is trying to kill us and our only option in an instant is to protect us in a way that could result in death to the other, that is satyagraha. All things being equal, in that instant it is our best unique action that is giving priority to the common good, to the natural force of truth.

Satyagraha, the natural force of truth, is giving priority to the natural primary good intention of every human being when relating with others as individuals, a group, or even as a nation. It is loving persuasion and invitation, or loving non-cooperation if necessary, to have all involved reconsider their position and change it to a more mature one that is now appropriate given our mutual ability to embrace the new more mature choice.

Nothing in my extensive reading of and about Gandhi reveals that he understood the relationship between language and reality and therefore of the importance of giving priority to priorities in his thinking. Therefore he accepted the term "non-violence" to describe satyagraha in English. Yet his behavior clearly reveals that he understood the importance of lovingly inviting maturation from a place of trust that the highest priority of every human being is the common good.

Life is Now Experienced as Meaningful

Also, when we have mastered the skill of the highest layer of maturity of the skill of self-consciousness life is at all times experienced as meaningful. We are *primarily self-conscious experience* and each moment we are able to identify the best unique thing we can do that is our direct participation in the natural and effortless maturation of the universe.

Allow me to point out that the discovery of this was the accomplishment of the goal of my first vow when a sophomore in high school and kneeling on the kneeler in the small chapel across from my locker at Creighton Prep. It only took me fifty-five years! One of my current eldering pleasures is sharing it with you.

What Does this Have to do with the Maturation of Capitalism into Common Good Capitalism?

So, you now might ask, what does all of this have to do with the maturation of capitalism into common good capitalism?

Currently to a great extent many of us living in our developed nations are operating at the Adult Layer of maturity in the skill of self-consciousness. We are giving priority to outside beliefs and, therefore, whether or not we are aware of it our most fundamental belief is that separate parts (time and space) are real. Many professional scientists also still believe this is true. It is not true.

Time and space (separate parts) are valuable, as valuable as the oneness of nature, but they are not real. They are a mutual illusion tool.

When our professional scientists learn they do not have to give up anything they have done or are doing but to only surround it with the fundamental truth that the universe is an indivisible whole, they will quickly and easily embrace it. They will see that both are *equally* valuable: time–space and oneness. So they do not have to give up one for the other as has been the assumption since they (we) used science to overthrow the king system. In their thinking they can now include both and fully and equally value both. The only thing they will be adding is the oneness pattern of thinking: they will give priority to the oneness of nature and second priority to time–space while valuing both equally.

Thus, this next layer in our maturation as a human species is the widespread discovery that this third of the three dimensions of the skill of self-consciousness represents a fact: the universe is an indivisible whole. It is also respecting that this is obviously self-evident if we each keep our power and primarily turn our attention to our direct experience. It is the honoring of our ability and right of full freedom by ending voluntary inside oppression (giving our power to any outside belief).

As a result of giving priority to personal science, full inside as well as outside freedom, there will be the full embrace of the fundamental inside belief that the universe is an indivisible whole: the inside belief at the Elder Layer. This will be occurring at the same time that it is discovered that not only is competition not the fundamental process in nature but also that *our major corporations are already primarily cooperating.* They are giving priority to rapidly creating near duopoly monopolies in every product area.

Once the above is well understood, corporate board members and executives will not only realize that making this change is how their duopolies can survive but also how all their employees, the communities where they exist, and everyone involved with their companies will fully enjoy working in and with them. They will also realize they are in the best position to provide the leadership desperately needed to mature the entire human species to not only understand the above but to also thereby solve all the problems that are the result of immature behaviors in the past, such as ending poverty, war, and environmental destruction.

They will realize that, relative to one another, agreements with their duopoly partner and the other competitors for the common good of all is legal and will not cost them a penny: if necessary they will each raise their prices equally as they have already been doing. Then competition on price and in every other way will continue as before. It will not only increase their profitability appropriately but also sustain it. And all involved in or with their two companies will experience the joy of having their *priority* be the common good. Profit to sustain being able to serve in this way is now second in priority and can probably and nearly always be adequate.

Executives will take lower salaries, only as much as necessary in some cases, because they will see that as also a contribution to the common good. They and everyone else will begin viewing themselves as trustees of the wealth and power they posses instead of the owners of it. As a result they will begin to think in terms of freely choosing to keep only what they need and manage the rest for the common good.

Oh, some will think at this point that the legal highest priority of companies is to give priority to the financial interests of their shareholders. So they cannot change to give priority to the common good. From two directions it is clear that this is not true.

First and the main reason, if a company is part of a *society* they have agreed to give priority to the common good. To do otherwise for any reason is to leave the society and be in competition with it. Therefore, any law is secondary to this. No mature judge is going to find a company guilty of breaking any law if they give priority to the common good instead of self-interest. Also, collusion for self-interest is illegal, but independent action and cooperation for the common good is not only legal but also encouraged by nearly all governments.

Second, if giving priority to the common good increases the financial return to the shareholders, particularly the security of their investments and the ability to sustain a profit, technically and legally it is accurately perceived as *increasing the financial interests of the shareholders.* By having the financial return second in priority, sustainable profitability is more secure and the potential for a consistent reasonable and appropriate level is enhanced.

So from either perspective this prioritization enhances the financial benefit to the shareholders.

In addition, there is no legal basis for giving priority to the financial return to shareholders above all else. No national or state law requires it. It is true that courts have given it priority when companies are being bought and at other times.

When my team in 2000 was attempting to buy Ben & Jerry's, the board voted to sell it to us for $38 a share even thought there was an outstanding offer from Unilever to buy it for $40 a share. We knew the minority shareholders would sue us and we wanted them to sue us. Since most of the shareholders were Vermonters who wanted Ben & Jerry's to remain in Vermont, we were hoping that the judge would allow the sale to us. If so a social reason would be given priority over the purchase price. Our hope was that this would set a precedent that a social concern could be given priority over a higher financial offer.

It never went to court. Someone informed Nestlé that Ben & Jerry's was about to sign papers selling their company to my group. Nestlé then offered a significantly higher price. We knew the price difference would not allow the judge to find in our favor. We withdrew our offer and eventually made arrangements with Unilever to buy it and sign a unique contract with Ben & Jerry's.

Besides keeping all the social agreements we had negotiated with Unilever when they were going to be our minority partner, Ben & Jerry's would remain a separate company inside Unilever. It also obligated them to allow us to forever spend annually the same percentage of the budget on social activism as was spent the year we were bought. The board, now with me on it, would remain in existence and its membership would be self-perpetuating. Its primarily responsibility is to assure this contract is kept. We are also responsible for guiding the social mission and brand integrity of Ben & Jerry's.

We cut a very good deal. We got Unilever's global distribution system that was essential, everything we wanted in terms of how the company would be operated in the future, and we didn't have to buy the company.

Until the 1970s corporate America had a strong sense that their highest priority was the common good. For instance, Robert Wood Johnson, the founder of Johnson & Johnson, practiced and promoted "managerial capitalism," as he called it: customers first, workers second, managers third, communities fourth, and shareholders fifth. Until the 1980s the Roundtable, an association of large US corporations and banks, honored that the primary responsibility of corporations was the common good. It now declares "The principle objective of a business enterprise is to generate economic returns to its owners."

It was Milton Friedman, a laissez-faire economics professor from the University of Chicago, who is given the most credit for changing this starting in the 1970s. Ever since it has been pushed so hard by professors, CEOs, lobbyists, and the news media that it is now assumed to be conventional wisdom. It is not wisdom. It is an aberration. A deviation from a moral standard. Fundamentally it comes from the acceptance of separate parts as real and, therefore, one of them must be given priority and all the others must yield to it. (*The Hightower Lowdown*, Volume 18, Number 2, February 2016)

Common good capitalism is a return to a moral standard in business *that is also based on full rather than partial freedom*. Competitors meet, with two or more non-voting government officials and citizen representatives present, and freely reach agreements that give priority to the common good. Their continued competition everywhere else is now their second priority.

Ben & Jerry's contract with Unilever has allowed us to give priority to the common good and second priority to profit. As mentioned earlier, Unilever, the third largest consumer products company on Earth, is also its largest ice cream company. It has many brands in many nations around the world.

Consistently, Ben & Jerry's is by far their most profitable brand.

People may or may not support the social changes we work to affect, for instance getting money out of politics, providing GMO labeling, the right of gays to marry, and responsible environmental behavior by all. However they like the fact that we are working to make the world a better place. We also make sure we have the best ice cream able to be produced. *The result is we have pricing power.* Each time we have raised our price we have studied to determine if it has affected sales. It never has. Thus, because we make the best ice cream and are giving priority to the common good, *we can sustain a strong profit.* Of course, it is also our responsibility to determine the profit that is appropriate within giving priority to the common good.

Finally, our corporations had little choice but to become near duopoly monopolies. When it became clear because of the easy and quick access to information that this was the next layer of maturity in the marketplace, if they did not cease the opportunity to become a duopoly two other companies would. Therefore it was accurately seen as necessary to survive.

Today it does not make any difference if there are two or ten companies that are dominant in a product market, cooperation is the fundamental process in nature so they will naturally give priority to cooperating either for their collective self-interest or for the common good. These are the only two choices before us now.

There are not really "good guys" and "bad guys" in this story or any story. There are only more mature and less mature guys. Whether or not people are aware of it, individual and collective maturation is the main game in town and it has always been and always will be the main game in town.

Once the above is understood and executives realize that it is all wins if they simply mature their thinking to be in alignment with at least the Elder Layer, the maturation of capitalism into common good capitalism will rapidly begin to occur.

Recall that in the editorial in the Introduction I described how Paul Polman, the CEO of Unilever, is turning it, the third largest consumer goods company on Earth, into a unilateral common good corporation modeled on Ben & Jerry's, even cooperating with competitors to do things such as working to save the rain forests in South America. His next step will be to arrange a sports league relationship with his competitors in each product market, called "cooperative competition" that will be described in the next chapter. More companies will unilaterally and in cooperation with their competitors move in this direction each day. Maturation is natural and unable to be easily resisted once it is known and experienced.

However, and this is very important to emphasize, it can only genuinely occur *and be successfully sustained* as the result of individuals understanding the importance of giving priority to personal science, *of each personally achieving full freedom.* They will have to have the courage to keep their power, all of it, and primarily go to their direct experience to determine what is their fundamental belief.

They will have to end the unconscious pattern of voluntary inside oppression by giving their power to a second thing, a freely chosen outside belief. They will have to know the importance of keeping their power—all of it—and using it to study their direct experience to identify their fundamental inside belief.

Only then will they become aware of the *wisdom* at the Elder Layer that will allow them to become one of the successful pioneers of our maturation of capitalism into common good capitalism. If they also mature into a mastery of the skill of the Mature Elder Layer, each moment they will also experience the *joy* of doing it.

By the way, for sixty years the scientific community believed human language was the result of a genetic mutation and, therefore, it was something biological in our brains. We now know it is a tool, called an "artifact" in the scientific community. It is a tool we learn the skill of using. However, unlike a hammer, it is a mutually agreed upon illusion tool. In Tom Wolfe's recent best-seller, The Kingdom of Speech, with great delight he tells the play-by-play story from Charles Darwin on of this reversal of position in the scientific community.

Thus, it is now ready to honor the fact that there are layers of smaller skills that build on one another and accumulate into the mature skill of using this tool of human language that allows us to be self-conscious. In addition, to also honor that at the higher layers of maturity of using it we naturally, effortlessly, and freely choose not only moral behavior but also give priority to the eldering of our children, each other, and our agreements as the activity of mature self-interest.

5
Common Good Capitalism Movement

IF WE CAN *IMAGINE* IT, IF IT IS *POSSIBLE*, AND IF IT IS *GOOD,* THEN we will eventually create it. Maturation is the fundamental process in nature.

Therefore we have three initial tasks.

The first task is to *imagine* a way we can mature capitalism into common good capitalism. We want our main strategy to be to build a movement because we want to use care, love, and invitation to mature something in the way we all think. Primarily this is about creating a freely chosen and more maturation consensus in the thinking of us all.

Second, we have to know it is identifying the next layer of maturity in the skill of self-consciousness that many are ready and able to understand so we can know it is now *possible* to build such a movement. This will have this maturation be realistic rather than idealistic.

Third, we want to build on rather than in any way qualify true full freedom. Therefore this design must be an option in the private sector one can choose, reject, or ignore. This would be a *good* way to do it.

Such an option has been created and will be described below. You will have to decide if you think it is a possible pathway or, if not, allow me to encourage you to present another route. There could be many routes occurring at the same time. Below I will only present the one I have identified.

Next, we need to make it available for others to consider. Concerning the one I am presenting, this has also already been accomplished. We have created a website where any individual and organization, for-profit or non-profit, can publicly declare that his, her, or its highest priority is the common good and second priority is profit or mission. The website is www.commongoodcapitalism.org. Allow me to encourage you to go to it and join as an individual (free) and to also have all the organizations of which you are an employee or member join (An annual fee of your choice is requested and it could be as small as a dollar. The purpose is to provide an opportunity for organizations to continuously fund this movement at whatever level they choose.).

This website was the result of a talk I gave in the Social Business Class at the Isenberg School of Business at the University of Massachusetts in November of 2014. I noticed that the eyes of three students had been wide open with excitement as I described how capitalism was going to mature into common good capitalism.

So at the end of my presentation I pointed out that Bill McKibben came up with the idea of creating the 350.org website while speaking to one of his classes at Middlebury College. He proposed that they set it up with that name as a way to raise the awareness of people around the world of the importance of not going over 350 parts per million of carbon in the air, the amount beyond which would be very dangerous for the healthy survival of human life on Earth. They would simply ask people to take some kind of action to alert others to this danger and send a picture and story about it to the website creators. So many did it that the organization has emerged as one of the most powerful environmental organizations on Earth by recently advocating that people and institutions divest from investments in companies that produce fossil fuels. It is having significant success.

I then pointed out that we could launch the Common Good Capitalism Movement website to see if we could also stimulate interest in building a movement around it. I invited anyone who was interested in helping me do that to come up and talk to me afterwards. Those exact three students came forward, as well as the instructor, Chetan Chawla. The three students were Sonam Serpa, Samantha Marino, and Vince Kozica. We began meeting nearly weekly and the website, primarily created by Vince's friend Ashleigh Syphers who joined our team, is now up and running.

Many organizations are already giving priority to the common good and they are not receiving recognition for doing it. For instance, many organizations, particularly local organizations, experience themselves as very embedded in their local communities and give priority to the common good, second priority to profit or mission, and doing well as a result. People value them and are very loyal to them. I am very familiar with this.

As mentioned earlier, I grew up in my father's meat market in South Omaha, Nebraska, Mollner's Meat Market. My father, Hienie, and his two brothers, Emerick and Leo who worked for him, were second generation Austrian-Hungarians. Their father, Albert, had journeyed at the age of seventeen from the small peasant village of Apetlon in Austria to the equivalent of the "New Apetlon" established by many others who had come to Omaha before him to work on building the railroads. He eventually used the skill he had learned as a teenager in his father's meat market to establish Mollner's Meat Market. When he died, my father took over the running of it. All six of us, his children, worked in the meat market from the age of seven until we graduated from college.

My father primarily sold love. He only secondarily sold meat.

Mollner's Meat Market was more of a clubhouse than a meat market. Everyone in New Apetlon knew that they survived by giving business to each other. We bought our groceries from Stiles Grocery, our hardware from Schneider's Hardware, our bakery from Ferd's Bakery, our drugs from Lyman's Pharmacy, and our beers from Al Nick's Bar.

When they tore down a block of houses in our Austrian-Hungarian neighborhood and built a Safeway grocery store, for decades we all acted like it did not exist. All remained loyal to our New Apetlon.

Today New Apetlon does not exist. Nearly all the New Apetlons do not exist. We now live in a global village. However there are still many organizations, for-profit and non-profit, that as best they can are giving priority to the common good and second priority to profit or mission and not receiving recognition for doing so.

The first goal of this movement is to bring attention to these organizations. They deserve to be recognized as common good organizations. We are hoping that the website will provide one way for this to begin to occur.

The second goal is to stimulate a conversation among us all on the question, "When people reach the higher layers of maturity in the skill of self-consciousness, do they freely choose to give priority to their self-interest or the common good?" We are confident that we will build toward a consensus on the conclusion that we already, naturally, and freely choose to give priority to the common good as best we understand how to do it. This priority is also not in competition with self-interest but enhances our ability to enjoy personal fulfillment.

As we mature into what I have described in the last chapter as the Elder and Mature Elder Layers of maturity in the skill of self-consciousness we will also become aware that the only way to achieve the experience of personal fulfillment is to discover full freedom. We will then insist upon keeping our power thereby ending all self-conscious and unconscious paternalism, the voluntary giving of our power to a second thing. When we then use our power to do a direct study of our immediate experience, we will eventually discover that it is abundantly self-evident that the universe is an indivisible whole.

Only then will it make sense to self-consciously choose to give priority to the common good of the one indivisible whole of which we are a part. Doing so will then eventually become a habit and our response to the emergence of duopoly monopolies will represent our maturation into the Elder Layer.

We will also understand that this enhances rather than reduces our personal experience of the joy of the fundamental feeling of happiness. As with our physical bodies, where we all currently assume oneness, we discover that what is best for the whole is also always best for each of the parts (in this case, for our physical bodies more fun and fewer enemies).

The third goal is to reveal to all who come to the website that there is a way, on a voluntary basis and fully within the private sector, to mature capitalism into common good capitalism. Even with the full support of Wall Street. Currently few imagine this is possible. It is not only possible it is also probably inevitable. In videos and few words the website reveals to all how it can rapidly happen and soon. (You want to particularly watch the four-minute video on the homepage.)

Allow me to encourage you to remember as you read further that maturation is the fundamental process in nature and it cannot be stopped. There are always setbacks, but the continuous fundamental direction cannot be stopped. Many are ready to mature into the Elder and Mature Elder Layers of maturity in the skill of self-consciousness. Once a higher layer of maturity in this skill is discovered it is naturally, effortlessly, and fully embraced because it always results in a greater sense of inner joy and peace: the self-conscious experience of the joy of the fundamental feeling of happiness as the container within which we experience everything else.

According to the pathway presented here, there are five options of membership in the Common Good Capitalism Movement.

Each is a way to make a greater commitment to building the common good capitalism community and it is possible to choose only one or more of them.

The names of them are:

Membership
Common Good Capitalism Certified
1-10% Club
Cap Club
Cooperative Competition

MEMBERSHIP

Any individual and for-profit or non-profit organization around the world can choose to become a member by going to the website and signing up.

In doing so they are publicly declaring that they are keeping the agreement we all make when we join any human society: to give priority to the common good. The purpose of this activity is to eventually expose to the public light those who are not willing to make this declaration. It is also to allow those who do publicly declare it to find each other for the purpose of forging cooperative agreements for the common good.

The people and organizations making this public declaration are joining with the others that, as members of our now global human society, are accepting responsibility for giving priority to the common good. They are also declaring that they are aware that if they do not choose the common good as their priority they have left our now global human society and are in competition with it.

Those who become members are publicly declaring that they are giving priority to the common good *as they determine it to be.* A definition of the common good is not presented. This is intentional.

What is the common good is constantly maturing. There was a time when killing, theft, and slavery were acceptable. Today nearly all societies on Earth do not allow killing, theft, and slavery within their own societies and, except when at war, in relationship with other societies. It is not yet universal but we are confident that it will someday be universal in the same way that learning a language is universal and agreeing that the Earth is round is universal. Also, the fact that their needed to be a Civil Rights, Women's and Environment Movements reveals the common good consensus continues to mature.

There are some issues that are still fully in debate but moving toward becoming universal. In the world of economic activity, one is "Should the minimum wage be a livable wage?"

Another is, "Should organizations, particularly for-profit competitors, directly cooperate with each other to reach agreements for the common good?" Some still see this cooperation as against competition that they perceive as the fundamental process in nature.

Organizations are already doing cooperation as a collective *defensive* position: competitors are creating associations to protect their industries and where appropriate agreeing on standards they will all follow. However many are not yet ready to execute collective *offensive* actions with each other on how they run their businesses for the common good of all.

"Should organizations give priority to the sustainability of the environment?" Some still think the parts of the environment are to be primarily used for self-interest and each of the parts of nature is responsible for taking care of itself as if we are not connected and interdependent with each other.

"Should an organization care about its effect upon the people who live around its production facilities?" If we are all separate from one another, they are seen by some as responsible for taking care of themselves in a competitive fight for survival.

As we mature as societies we will reach broad agreement on the answers to these questions.

Should a Company Give Priority to the Common Good or the Financial Interests of its Shareholders?

Here is another very important question where there is still a lack of broad agreement:

"Should a company give *priority* to the common good or the financial interests of its shareholders?" Again, this is operating on the assumption that the financial interests of shareholders are separate from our interdependence with nature. As stated earlier, some even think they are obligated to do this because of the laws of the state within which they are established, for-profit corporate law.

Because this is such an important issue for so many, let's take a second look at this question, "Should a company give priority to the common good or the financial interests of its shareholders?" Many believe that by law the highest priority of a for-profit company has to be the financial interests of its shareholders. It can be argued, as was argued earlier, that from two directions this is not true. Since the answer to this question is so important to many people, for emphasis allow me to repeat my answers to this question.

The first one is the fundamental argument of this book. If a person is a member of a human society, regardless of how it is structured, one has declared that his, her, or its organization's priority is the common good of the society. To not give priority to the common good is to leave the human society and be in competition with it. Thus if the desire is to remain a member of the society, the financial interests of the shareholders is second in priority.

However it can also be argued that it is in the best financial interests of the shareholders to give priority to the common good, especially as human societies mature into understanding that the universe is an indivisible whole: the Elder Layer of the skill of self-consciousness. To be seen as not doing so, especially as the public becomes aware of the consistent increase in the number of duopoly monopolies, can bring negative judgments toward the organization that is definitely not good for the financial interests of the shareholders. Also if by giving priority to the common good the company is more valued by all, especially its customers, this priority enhances its ability to survive and thrive. Therefore, honoring its priority as a member of a society can enhance the safety of its investors' capital and can more easily provide a steady good profit.

Thus, from either point of view it is financially beneficial to the shareholders for companies to give priority to the common good.

Common Good as well as Financial Audits

In addition, successful movements bring about maturation in the way we all think. As we mature into the Elder Layer of the skill of self-consciousness, customers will make a new demand of the companies that serve them. They will not only demand that their companies declare their highest priority is the common good but they will also want to know that their behavior reveals that they are actually doing it. And if the companies in a product market have forged some common good agreements, they will want to know the degree to which each company is keeping its agreement.

Thus, all will demand third party common good audits.

This will provide an honest evaluation of the company's relationships with their employees, suppliers, customers, environment, and the communities where they are active. This will allow the public and other companies to trust what each company is reporting. It is also a way for the company to learn where their giving of priority to the common good could use improvement. As they make these improvements the respect for the company will increase. Many companies, Ben & Jerry's being one, already provide internal generated or third party common good audits.

All other things being equal, those companies that are first to the market with this maturation process will be big winners financially. So giving priority to the common good will be discovered to be in the financial interests of the shareholders. They will be out in front and leading our inevitable collective maturation into this next layer of maturation in the skill of self-consciousness.

Ben & Jerry's is an excellent example of a common good company, even since being bought by Unilever. Since the beginning of the company when started in the 1970s by Ben Cohen and Jerry Greenfield, it has given priority to the common good and second priority to profit. It has spent a significant portion of its annual budget on social activism, educating the public about the importance of caring about the environment and communities. The result is its loyal customers, much as with Mollner's Meat Market's customers, love the company.

In the annual Wall Street polls in the 1990s, Ben & Jerry's was consistently voted the most socially responsible company in the USA. As mentioned earlier, when bought by Unilever in 2000, a contract was signed that has allowed it to each year in the future spend on social activism the same percentage of its annual budget as the year it was bought. And our board, which is self-perpetuating, was given responsibility for making sure this occurs. If Unilever fails to do this, we can sue them for breach of this contract.

The result is that Ben & Jerry's is the first common good corporation inside a multinational.

This was done because the Unilever executives at the time recognized that this was an essential part of what made the brand so loved and sales so successful. Unilever, the largest ice cream company on Earth, had twice tried to establish a super premium ice cream brand and had failed. They realized that Ben Cohen and Jerry Greenfield were onto something and did not want to mess with a winning hand in what they saw as this marketplace poker game.

To their continued astonishment, Ben & Jerry's, under this agreement, has continued to be by far their most financially successful ice cream brand. Whether people agree or disagree with its social activist positions, they continue to buy the ice cream. It is the best ice cream in the world; however Unilever makes many of the best ice creams in the world. Is it just a fluke, people's affection for an ice cream company created by a couple of Vermont hippies? Or is it because people respect a company that boldly and publicly declares each day that its highest priority is the common good through the social activism positions it takes and the money it spends to further them?

I believe it is the latter reason. Few people remember the history of Ben & Jerry's; however they are very aware of its current very public efforts to get money out of politics, get laws passed that require GMO labeling, fight for what is now called "climate justice," and support the rights of gays to marry. Customers may or may not support some or even all of the company's political positions, but that does not appear to affect the sales of the ice cream. Instead it reveals that they respect Ben & Jerry's for being an active participant in making the world a better place for us all.

And the company has also continued to be celebrated for giving priority to the common good. In 2006 Ben & Jerry's was ranked Number One in the USA in Corporate Social Responsibility based on the annual Golin Harris CSR Report.

This is supported by the love the consuming public has for many of the other companies that have chosen to give priority to the common good: Patagonia, Stonyfield, Calvert, Pax World, Cliff Bar, Prosperity Candle, Bright Horizons, and many others.

What is the result? Unilever is now taking notice of this and Paul Polman, the new CEO, is moving the entire global $60 billion dollar company, the third largest consumer products company on Earth with factories in a majority of its countries, toward giving priority to the common good in all it does. For instance, it has made a commitment to source product from two million small farmers by 2020. More than half of the agricultural materials it uses now come from sustainable sources and it has helped train 800,000 farmers to grow crops responsibly. It is even exploring becoming one of the first multinationals to receive B-Corp certification, a third party certification that its behavior is operating at a high level of social responsibility.

Is this evidence that the consuming public is maturing into the Elder Layer? I think so. Is it also evidence that some multinational corporations are taking notice and getting out in front of this natural maturation of our thinking? I think so. For instance, the September 1, 2015 issue of *Fortune* provided its first Change the World List, a list of 51 for-profit companies with projects focused on tackling "the world's most intransigent problems."

COMMON GOOD CAPITALISM CERTIFIED

This is a certification that indicates the company has become a member and has been certified by a third party, B-Lab, Inc. or another such as Green America Certification, that it is operating at a certain level of "common good behavior."

The only difference between being B-Corp Certified and being Common Good Certified is that the company has also publicly declared that its highest priority is the common good.

B-Corp Certification is a *checklist* of responsible behaviors. Common Good Certification is an indication of the company's *highest priority*.

Enron passed the social screens of many socially responsible certifying organizations. Yet their highest priority, as latter determined by the courts, was clearly not the common good. Were they lying? Or were they actually behaving socially responsibly in each of the areas being evaluated but giving priority to something very different from the common good?

The work that B-Corp, Green America, and other third party certification programs are doing is extremely valuable, essential, and fully supported by the Common Good Capitalism Movement. A third party certification process around the many particular areas of corporate behavior is needed and that is what they are providing.

However, at this time it is also essential that we go one step further and determine whether or not a company's publicly declared highest priority is the common good rather than the financial self-interests of a few. Could they lie? Yes. However now they have publicly declared it. Enron was living in a world where they judged it was natural and best to give priority to self-interest. They were just seeking socially responsible certification to support this priority.

This is why a company's public declaration that they are giving priority to the common good is so important: it is a clear and public break from this immature past, what is labeled "neo-liberalsim" by economists, the belief it is natural to give priority to self interest.

This is what a movement is. It is a declaration that what is currently a socially acceptable behavior is no longer acceptable. Not because there is a better option but because it is more than immature, it is immoral: a legal crime. It is not giving priority to the common good. Therefore we have to stop doing it to continue on the path of maturation.

The primary purpose of a fundamental movement is to mature the way we all think about something. Secondly, it is asking people to publicly declare that they have made the change. Thirdly, it is changing all of their behavior to be in support of this change. And, fourthly, for a business organization it is having a creditable third party publicly certify that their company is behaving at a certain level of common good behavior in all they do. B-Corp, Green America, and other organizations provide the latter and, in the eyes of the public, are essential to the success of this movement.

No company that becomes a member of the Common Good Capitalism Movement needs to become B-Corp Certified or certified by any other third party. It can be costly, especially for small organizations. However, any company that becomes a member of the Common Good Capitalism Movement and has also received B-Corp Certification, Green America Certification, or certain other certifications can also receive Common Good Certification. It is not necessary to be Common Good Certified to participate in any of the other membership activities of the Common Good Capitalism Movement.

This is a second way a company can become more actively involved in perpetuating this movement. So, especially if you are already certified as a B-Corp or other such certification, do consider having your organization become Common Good Certified as well.

1-10% CLUB

This is a third option an organization, for-profit or non-profit, can choose to support the emergence of the Common Good Movement. It can declare that somewhere between one and ten percent of their annual net profit (or positive cash flow in the case of a non-profit) will be invested (not donated) in Common Good Investment Banking Firms (CGIBF). The priority of the latter is to buy companies and convert them into Cap Club companies, described below.

The investors will receive a market rate of return on these investments; however, with a portion of these assets it may choose to receive a below market rate of return, especially in low income and more challenging areas of the world, to be more strongly supportive of this movement. (The Calvert Foundation, described below, is one organization that provides this investment option: www.calvertfoundation.org.)

It is important to provide the capital necessary to build this movement. This is a way an organization can participate in doing so in a way that also supports their organization by receiving a market rate return on its investment.

Foundations could also be supportive by investing a portion of their endowment capital in common good investment banking firms. Many will emerge around the world and investors will be able to choose the one or a number of them in which to invest.

CAP CLUB

This is for for-profit organizations that also choose to place a cap on their annual return (total of dividend and stock appreciation) to equity investors.

The level of cap is not what is most important. What is most important is that it be made public. This will allow society to participate in deciding if the cap is appropriate.

For instance, if a company is a start-up the annual cap can be 1,000%. As the company matures, it can lower its cap. However, if the company is one of a near duopoly monopoly, it should appropriately be somewhere below a 15% annual return to shareholders.

The principle is the ancient one: rather than an unlimited upside investors deserve a financial return that is reasonable relative to their risk.

In this way, by choosing an appropriate cap, the chosen priority is the common good. The company will now be free to operate under these priorities and also free of pressure to give priority to seeking the highest return possible to shareholders, only the level to which they have committed. Of course, near duopoly monopolies will have one of the lower caps. Each year they would invest any annual excess profit over their cap in CGIBFs.

The only use of the assets invested in CGIBFs would be to use them as collateral to borrow money during difficult times or to grow the business. If borrowed on, the annual interest cost and realized or unrealized gain (from interest, dividend income and/or equity appreciation) could be similar. Thus the capital is able to serve both purposes at no significant cost to the company. (Mondragon in the Basque region of Spain has used this approach of having capital artfully go in two directions at the same time.)

COOPERATIVE COMPETITION

This is the fifth way members can participate in common good capitalism. It is also the main purpose for launching the Common Good Capitalism Movement. It is graduating our business behavior into the Elder Layer of maturity of the human skill of self-consciousness.

Competitors in each product market reach agreements that give priority to the common good and secondly continue to compete as ferociously as before: the sports league model.

Fortunately, the near duopolization of product markets will make this easier to accomplish. When we, the public, become aware of it, we will feel trapped. We want the companies to continue providing the products and services that we need. On the other hand, monopoly behavior is not acceptable. Therefore, eventually we will demand a solution that ends this monopoly behavior.

Common good capitalism is the only solution to all the immaturities of capitalism that everyone will eventually support. It builds on individual freedom and free markets. These are two behaviors we do not want to end or limit accept through voluntary agreements where the priority is the common good. This solution is voluntary action to do so that also allows the public to participate in determining what it is for our time.

Therefore, it is inevitable. Speeding up this inevitability is the primary goal of the Common Good Capitalism Movement.

Here is the Vision, Mission and Guiding Principles of this movement:

Vision

To create a world where, like the teams of sports leagues, competitors in each product market voluntarily meet; they agree on employee, community, and environment policies that give priority to the common good; they provide annual common good audits so the public can be in on-going conversations with the companies as to what improvements in the common good agreements are appropriate for our time; and, like the teams in sports leagues, they secondly compete as ferociously as before only now within voluntary "common good rules of play."

Mission

To build a Common Good Capitalism Movement to bring about the above vision.

Guiding Principles

1. It is natural for people to mature to where they freely choose to give priority to the common good, known through the ages as "moral behavior."
2. Giving priority to anything other than the common good is "immoral behavior": the priority is self-interest at the expense of the common good.
3. All societies, regardless of how they are structured, continuously create laws to assure that all activities give priority to the common good.
4. Individuals and organizations within societies that are not giving priority to the common good have left the society and are now in competition with it.
5. It is currently believed by many in the business community that it is acceptable to give priority to the financial interests of their shareholders. This is immoral. Doing so is leaving the society and being in competition with it.
6. Therefore, a movement needs to emerge that educates the public of the immorality of this priority until all businesses freely choose to give priority to the common good, both unilaterally and in associations with their competitors, so there is no longer acceptance of this immoral priority in the business community.

While preserving and building on individual freedom and free markets, Common Good Capitalism is a solution to the immaturities of capitalism where all will experience themselves as winning.

It is the *sports league model* used by children's soccer leagues and professional leagues such as the National Basketball Association (NBA). There the competitors meet, reach agreement on the "common good rules of play," and provide officials to make sure the agreements are continuously given priority while the teams ferociously compete as their second priority. Herein this is labeled "cooperative competition."

In the business community, both locally and internationally, this model can be used to voluntarily give priority to the common good. The competitors in each product market can meet, agree on the "common good rules of play," each provide an annual common good audit as well as a financial audit also by creditable third parties, and then continue to ferociously compete as their second priority.

Now, as with sports leagues, the highest priority in the business community is the common good in a way that all involved experience themselves as winning:

Shareholders
- public anger at duopoly monopoly behavior ends
- a consistent and appropriate financial return is more easily achieved
- they know their financial return is not at the expense of the common good
- relative to one another it will not cost the companies a penny: any necessary increase in costs is raised by all competitors at the same time

Employees
- they know their contribution is primarily in the service of the common good
- their minimum compensation is what is voluntarily determined by all involved to be appropriate for the common good and it is with all competitors in their product market association
- they are equal participants with all involved in making these agreements

Consumers, Venders, & Politicians
- they know the freely chosen priority of all involved is the common good of all human beings and nature

Citizenry & All Involved

– the process is open and transparent so all are equal participants in the discussions of what is giving priority to the common good for the entire society, not just the shareholders and employees

– the third party common good audits provide verification that all participants are giving priority to the common good in their agreements and that their behavior is consistently honoring those agreements

As we now know the Information Age has made it easier for businesses to cooperate with their competitors to give priority to their collective self-interest. Without ever talking to each other they can primarily do it by matching each other's fundamental price increases. They experience this as legal behavior because they are not breaking the laws against direct communication for this purpose. Therefore, all competitors have determined they must seek a duopoly monopoly in each of their product markets. Since it is now determined by the response of society to be legal, if they do not pursue it two other companies will eventually achieve it. So they have to pursue it or it is deemed wise to exit that market and focus on the products in the markets where this can be achieved.

This duopolization of each product market, where a few and maybe only two companies control more than 80% of a product market, is the priority on Wall Street and the other financial centers around the world. Here again are some of the very visible duopoly monopolies in the USA: CVS-Walgreens, Home Depot-Lowe's, MasterCard-Visa, Coca Cola-Pepsi, UPS-Fed Ex.

This sports league solution will also allow these near duopoly or whatever monopolies to continue in existence with other competitors always free to join their product market association. Or if they choose to not join they will be easily exposed to the public as not doing so. Increasingly this will not be acceptable by the public and, therefore, their business could have significant challenges.

Most important, the companies will no longer operate at the expense of the employees, community, and environment. Instead they will voluntarily make decisions that give priority to the common good of the society, now

increasingly a global society.

The publicly shared common good audits, the equivalent of the referees in the sports league model, allow all to be in an on-going conversation on what is the appropriate way for our time to give priority to the common good. As the Civil Rights, Women's, and Environment Movements reveal, we are continuously maturing in our understanding of what is giving priority to the common good.

For instance, in each production location the companies can agree to have the minimum wage be the livable wage. They can agree on worker benefits and other employee issues, and where unions exist these agreements are now across all competitors in a product area. They can agree on environment and safety standards. They can even agree to donate the same percentage of annual net profit to organizations working to end poverty. Also, the common good audits will allow all the competitors and the public to trust that all are keeping their agreements.

The companies are now common good companies, companies that voluntarily give priority to the common good and second priority to the financial interests of the shareholders.

Finally, this is voluntary action in the private sector. Competitors are free to do or not do it and they create the process and agreements. It is also legal; all governments encourage cooperation for the common good. It is direct collusion for self-interest that is illegal. Also, because it is clearly giving priority to the common good, appropriate legislation in support of this solution will eventually be passed that nearly all will support.

This forging of agreements among competitors can occur at the local level as well as at the national and international level. For instance, local businesses such as restaurants can reach agreement to pay their help an agreed upon minimum wage that would end the low pay to undocumented workers.

This solution is the only solution that both honors individual freedom and builds on and sustains free markets. So it is the solution that will eventually be chosen. The primary purpose of the Common Good Capitalism Movement is to have it happen sooner rather than later.

By going to the Common Good Capitalism Movement website (www. commongoodcapitalism.org) and becoming a member of this community, individuals and organizations can publicly declare that they are now committed to giving priority to the common good. This will not only build this movement. It will also let others in your product area know you are ready to reach agreement with them to be a cooperative competitor.

So, if you agree it is time to build a movement to mature capitalism into common good capitalism allow me to encourage you to add your weight to this movement by going to the Common Good Capitalism Movement website and publicly declare it there. The most powerful source for maturation in a society is movements. Please consider adding your name (no cost for individuals but a request for a small annual contribution from businesses to cover costs) as a supporter of this movement.

We have now created five options that can allow for-profit and non-profit organizations to continuously support the growth of the Common Good Capitalism Movement: Membership, Common Good Certification, 1-10% Club, Cap Club, and Cooperative Competitors. It can choose one or more of them or none of them. All also has to be a free choice in the private sector.

What is most important is that the public becomes aware that there is a private sector path to finance the maturation of capitalism into common good capitalism.

80% of Investment Capital Seeks a 10–12% Return

Approximately 80% of investment capital is searching for a 10–12% annual return; only 20% is "hot money" looking for a quick and high return.

The goal of the Cap Club businesses is to eventually place their cap near this (for instance, 12%) and to consistently provide it. In addition they will give comfort to investors by building up a large body of retained assets that are invested in CGIBFs that back up their ability to continually provide this annual return. This will also attract strong consumer support for the company.

It will also attract the 80% of investment capital available in the market-place from endowments, pension funds, mutual funds, insurance companies, and the public.

Financial planners and asset managers will want the conservative portion of their clients' equity portfolios invested in these companies. Foundations can even provide the option of allowing donations to their endowments to have the dollars restricted to only be invested in Cap Club companies, common good investment funds or ETFs (electronic transfer funds), or CGIBFs, that is *only in common good securities.*

It is through this kind of financial activity by individuals and organizations that the building of the Common Good Movement will be self-financed and seen as eventually dominant on the planet. Then just as companies are becoming environmentally responsible, treating women and minorities equally, and providing health benefits to married gay couples because of those movement's success, they will rapidly convert to be common good corporations to become part of the ever growing success of the Common Good Movement.

So this is how individual and organization investors can actively part-icipate in supporting our maturation into common good capitalism.

Wall Street screamed in anger when the founders of Google, Larry Page and Sergey Brin, went public while they owned such a large pool of B Shares of ten votes per share so they maintained voting control of the company. Wall Street professionals currently believe their process, or whoever can amass a controlling interest in its shares, should control companies and that the highest priority should at all times be the maximization of the financial returns to shareholders. However Wall Street adjusted and other companies have done the same since.

In the same way Wall Street will adjust to the existence of companies that give priority to the common good.

In the world of mutual funds and ETFs, at this time the public can invest in what are currently called "responsible investment funds or ETFs" but I suspect they will eventually be called "common good investment funds or ETFs."

Another indication of our maturation into the Elder and Mature Elder Layers is the rapid growth of responsible mutual funds. In the late 1970s when I was at the Institute for Community Economics in Cambridge, I facilitated one of the first groups to write a set of social screens for investing when this industry did not exist. People saw only two things they could do with their savings: invest them or donate them. We presented a third option: responsible investing. This is where the investments are in companies that meet a minimum standard of responsible behavior in relationship with their employees, the environment, and the community. At that time it was our way of encouraging investors to move toward giving priority to the common good.

In 1982 a group of us used those social screens to create the first family of socially responsible mutual funds, the Calvert Family of Socially Responsible Mutual Funds, now known simply as the "Calvert Funds." A recent study by the Social Investment Forum (www.ussif.org) determined that today one in every six dollars professionally managed uses some form of social screens. In 1982 no one, even our supporters, thought we would be successful creating such a family of mutual funds. Today the Calvert Group has $12 billion under management and between 2012 and 2014 in the USA assets managed under responsible principles doubled to more that $6 trillion. Among Millennials, who will inherit more than $40 trillion over the next few decades, 92% believe that a business's purpose extends beyond profit.

Judith Rodin, in an article entitled *The End of Short-Termism* in *Fortune* magazine reports the following:

Current trends go beyond previous models of corporate social responsibility precisely because more companies see that a focus on social and environmental impact affects the bottom line. As a result, companies are reimagining how they source, operate, and innovate to advance a healthier planet and create more inclusive economies—those with more opportunities for more people—as part of a virtuous business circle.

For executives looking to take this approach, there's good news: You don't have to go it alone. There are models to learn from and emulate,...partners waiting to lend expertise, and more sophisticated systems for measuring and proving impact beyond financials. Socially responsible management is no longer the Wild West but the new normal. And in the near future, when you do what is right for your long term success by doing more good for the world, investors won't just give you permission—they'll reward you.

In addition and as stated earlier, recently BlackRock, the largest financial asset manager in the USA, revealed they are launching a series of "social funds." Also recently, Morningstar, the most prominent and respected evaluator of the performance of mutual funds, made a very important announcement. It provides a one to five star rating of the financial performance of mutual funds. Now for most of their mutual funds, both those that have and have not declared they endeavor to be socially responsible, they will provide a one to five globe rating of their socially responsible behavior. The globe will be a picture of the Earth.

Thus, mainstream investing is maturing into being socially responsible investing, today also labeled "impact investing."

What is making this easier for people to do is that for more than two decades it has financially performed as well as non-socially responsible investing. So financially there is nothing to lose in investing socially responsibly. Thus, when they see they can invest in companies that are making the world a better place rather than not and receive the same financial return, the greater enjoyment of participating in maturation for the common good has them naturally pulled toward doing it.

This is an excellent example of a *movement* that has succeeded in maturing something in the way we all think. This is changing everything else in its field. I give a large amount of the credit for this maturation of the Wall Street community to the Environment and Socially Responsible Investing Movements. In particular much of the credit goes to all those grade school teachers who taught our children to love, value, and seek to preserve our environment. Now that the Millennial Generation is inheriting more than $40 trillion the marketplace is responding. Here we can witness how movements are changing the consumers, they are changing the corporations, and all of this will eventually change the politicians.

All of the above is additional evidence that we are maturing into common good capitalism.

Global Development by Corporations

The only thing we know that reduces population growth is economic development. At the same time, increasingly each year we have college educated students in the developed countries who cannot find appropriate jobs. Now they can be provided with fun, interesting, and meaningful jobs in common good enterprises that are in the business of building free market common good economies in developing countries. This will not only provide more customers for all businesses but also reduce poverty and population growth.

There is also no better way for the developed world to deal with its unemployed college graduates and others while simultaneously rapidly assisting the developing world to mature its economies thereby providing more customers for all businesses.

I point this out because not only will the governments of developed nations discover that this is a solution to their growing unemployment problem, but I believe that eventually the common good corporate community will also want to provide leadership here, even unilaterally doing so as Ben & Jerry's has, to gain a competitive edge.

I can imagine a day when Intel, Google, Facebook, Netflix, and Pepsi each provide a guarantee (no capital outlay is necessary) to a private bank, or the World Bank, to secure a large loan of billions of dollars. With it they will also loan executives and special skill employees for the purpose of establishing companies in underdeveloped or developing nations. These companies will arrange with those governments to build in a mutually chosen location the infrastructure (roads, utilities, water and sewage systems, including a tax collection agency) and consumer businesses that establish a modern, free market and socially and environmentally responsible economy. They will hire many of the unemployed in the developing nations to reduce its unemployment and in the process train many in marketable skills.

When done and all the jobs have been successfully transferred to local people, the developing nation will issue government bonds to raise the capital to pay off the borrowed capital and be able to service them with the increased tax base. The corporation will then be released from its guarantee. Such a successful program will certainly also receive low interest capital and grants from international agencies like the World Bank and International Monetary Fund. They will also buy their bonds.

In particular, this is an excellent way for the duopoly monopoly companies to be allowed to maintain their duopolies. They will be seen as using their expertise to take a significant level of action for the common good at a low risk of financial cost because they have full control of the relationship with the developing nation.

In these kinds of ways the duopolies will eventually partially compete based on who is doing the most for the common good.

It will also become clear to all that there is a free market pathway to have access to the capital needed to mature our business communities around the world, capitalist and communist, into a global common good capitalism community. Eventually, as this more mature truth is widely embraced, businesses of all sizes will either be bought or convert into Cap Club businesses. All this will occur within the global free market economy and through voluntary action or, perhaps reluctantly at first, as the result of the need for businesses to survive in a marketplace driven by customer insistence on a forever maturing common good priority. Once this sustainable vision for the future is viewed as inevitable, the conversion of our multinational businesses into common good businesses could occur in a few years.

In 1970, how many participants in the first Earth Day on the Boston Common thought that we would be this far along in self-consciously managing the resources of the planet for the common good, with global meetings of nations attending to it? Yes, we have much further to go, but we are also much further along toward getting there. The Common Good Movement will definitely assist the Environment Movement toward its goal.

Indeed, think of the first person who noticed when a boat goes out to sea the bottom is the first part of the boat to disappear. And then, looking in both directions, also noticed that the horizon was a perfect half circle. As a result, that person discovered the truth that the Earth is not flat but round, just such a big round that it makes sense to act like it is flat when chopping vegetables or building a house. That person knew from *direct experience* it was true and was able each day to verify it as true in direct experience. That person also knew that someday all children would be born into a world where all agreed the Earth is round because it is true. That day has come.

Some of us now know from the keeping of our power, all of it, and using it to primarily study of our direct experience that the universe is an indivisible whole. However as the result of the creation of a human language that is always between whatever we are thinking or perceiving and us—that we treasure because it allows us to be self-conscious—we easily assume it is an immense number of separate parts like the words in our languages. Since it is true that it is an indivisible whole, *and we are able each day to verify this is true in direct experience,* we know that someday all will be born into a world that knows it is true.

That day has not come, but we now know that it will come.

While walking along a river, if we see a small child drowning, we know how to swim, and there is no one else around, we immediately jump into the water and bring the child to safety. This is often referred to as a "moral imperative," something so obvious for the common good that we are naturally compelled to do it.

Those of us who have become aware from an understanding of full freedom that the universe is an indivisible whole find ourselves in a similar situation. As a result we are jumping into the river to let everyone know in every way we can that the universe is an indivisible whole. By nature all of us are always giving priority to the common good, regardless of whether or not we are aware of it. It is not possible to do otherwise. That is the nature of all of us being parts of an indivisible whole. Thus, any beliefs we have had that do not honor this accurate fundamental inside known belief have been naturally and effortlessly dropped. We have directly observed that the universe is an indivisible whole, for us this is no longer just an idea but a fact, and we now know that some day every child will be born into a world that knows this is true because it is true.

And, while giving priority to the eternal now as we daily swim in the river of life, we want to do what we can to have everyone we meet discover the importance of keeping their power, then turning their primary attention to their direct experience, and becoming a fully free human being, a personal scientist. We are fully confident that they will then eventually discover what is self-evident there: the universe is an indivisible whole, not an immense number of separate and competing parts.

In addition, whatever we can do to assist others to discover full freedom and build organizations that honor the accurate fundamental inside belief we now know, we must do. For us it is now a moral imperative as strong and obvious to us as the need to jump into the river to save the drowning child.

Common Good Chapters

Someday all of us, including all in our capitalist and communist economies, will mature to where we "together freely, directly, and self-consciously choose to give priority to the common good." That day is not now. Therefore another way you can assist in the growth of this movement is to form a Common Good Chapter (CGC).

The reason people will want to form chapters is to stimulate the inevitable and widespread embrace of this new, more mature truth, so it occurs sooner rather than later.

I invite anyone interested in starting a local CGC in your community to go to our website, www.commongoodcapitalism.org. On the *About Us* menu, read the *Guidelines for Starting a CGC Chapter*. As more and more local organizations band together to build this movement, more and more of the larger organizations will judge that it is also wise to become a part of this movement.

This is how common good movements grow. They have to be based not only on a more mature truth but also on the next more mature truth many are now ready to embrace. As more and more individuals and organizations publicly embrace it, the movement grows. Eventually the maturation in the thinking of us all occurs.

A local chapter is a good way to invite other people and organizations, for-profit and non-profit, in your local community to become involved. A chapter can also organize local actions to encourage not only unilaterally giving priority to the common good but also the building of cooperative agreements among competitors. For instance, one of the actions we are considering locally is forging an agreement among all restaurants and fast food establishments to raise the minimum wage above that required by the state and closer to a livable wage.

Like the environmental movement, this organization will emerge from the bottom up based on agreement around this new more mature truth, or quite possibly, it will not emerge until later; but something along these lines will eventually emerge. Maturation cannot be stopped.

Responsible Investing

As briefly mentioned earlier, in the 1970s I was one of the many pioneers of what became known as "responsible investing." We were a bunch of hippies throwing pebbles at the big windows on the top floor of the corporate head-quarters and shouting, "Care more about the employees, the community, and the environment!"

From around the country Robert Swann and I, founders of the Institute for Community Economics (ICE), brought together fifteen leaders with social and financial expertise. Over eighteen months of monthly meetings we wrote arguably one of the first comprehensive set of social screens to guide investment decisions. Using those social screens, in 1982 Wayne Silby, one of the members I invited into that group, others, and I, created the Calvert Social Investment Funds (www.calvert.com), the first family of such funds, as a way for people to participate in this movement. Now, as mentioned earlier, around the world there are trillions invested with some form of social screens and it is now becoming mainstream.

Responsible investing was definitely a step forward. However, many of us now realize our naïveté, even though it was a significant step in the right direction.

We were focusing on the secondary priorities—a checklist of socially responsible behaviors—and ignoring the highest priority!

Common good capitalism focuses on the highest priority, the priority that all the other priorities primarily accommodate.

As revealed earlier in the comments about Enron, it is possible to have the highest priority be self-interest and be able to pass all of the social screens on the checklist.

What is always most important is an individual's or organization's highest priority.

It reveals the layer of maturity in the skill of self-consciousness at which he, she, or it is operating. That determines everything else that is chosen or done.

Today, in the USA, there are thousands of responsible mutual funds and ETFs; and there is $6.6 trillion invested sustainably in the US; more than what is invested in exchange-traded funds and hedge funds combined. The performance of the longest running social index, the KLD 400 Social Index, reveals that, all things being equal, it is not necessary to give up financial return when investing responsibly. It is now backed by decades of evidence: you don't have to give up performance to invest responsibly.

For the last twenty-three years the above index has nearly exactly tracked the S&P 500 Index and, over the last few years, is currently outperforming it.

Thus, if you have assets being managed by an asset manager I strongly encourage you to speak with him or her and ask that your investments be in responsible investment funds or ETFs. If you are managing your assets, I suggest you Google "socially responsible investment funds lists." This will bring up many organizations where you can learn about this area of investing. (I am a partner in a responsible asset management firm, Stakeholders Capital, Inc. You can learn more about us at our website: www.stakeholderscapital.com and our team will be happy to assist you.)

In the future I am confident there will be common good investment funds that invest in companies where the priority is the common good and they provide common good audits by creditable third parties.

Community Investing

Another movement, called "community investing," also began to take off in the 1970s. ICE was one of the pioneers of it as well. Eventually many such programs were created and became known as "community development financial institutions (CDFIs)." They are tax-exempt organizations that focus on raising donations and investment capital to invest in low-income housing developments, socially responsible businesses and cooperatives in low income communities, community land trusts, and microloan programs around the world (small uncollateralized loans to poor people to build a small business).

I remember writing up a loan contract on one side of a sheet of paper. It invited people to loan ICE any amount of money, and they could choose their interest rate between zero and 6%. We then put the capital in a separate checking account and lent it to some of the above organizations. In the 1990s the Clinton Administration and Congress passed a law for the U. S. Treasury to make grants and loans to CDFIs, which continues to this day. There is now a CDFI in nearly all of America's local, regional, or state communities.

At Calvert, in 1988, we began a program that eventually became the Calvert Foundation that now raises low cost investment capital from individuals and organizations. Investors can choose their interest rate between zero and two percent based on the length of the commitment of the capital. It is the only non-profit note able to be purchased by investment advisors on their computers the same way they purchase a stock, bond, or mutual fund. It is invested in hundreds of CDFIs in the USA and in microloan programs around the world. Today, with our billionth dollar now loaned, this capital is working to end poverty and improve our social and environmental fabric on every continent on the planet. (www.calvertfoundation.org).

Impact Investing

Today a new term has emerged. "Impact investing" is an umbrella term for any and all investments that to any degree include a social or environmental priority in its list of high priorities. This is also called "blended value" by my friend Jed Emerson who, with Antony Bugg-Levine, has written a book on it called *Impact Investing: Transforming How We Make Money While Making a Difference.*

This term, impact investing, is an easier term for a wider circle of people to comfortably use: it states a process instead of a value position. This allows anyone to project into it just about anything one wishes as long as it can be argued that it is giving some concern to making the world a better place. This has led to a significant growth of investments in the direction of common good investing. J.P. Morgan, Goldman Sachs, and Morgan Stanley, the three largest investment banks, now have impact investment programs. Impact investing now also defines the entire responsible investing area. This adds legitimacy to all the different responsible investing approaches that are now seen on a continuum of many different ways to invest and returns being sought.

Muhammad Yunus, winner of the 2006 Nobel Peace Prize for founding the Grameen Bank in Bangladesh and one of the pioneers of microloans, has launched a program he calls "social business." It does not provide a financial return to investors. Thus, he has established the farthest end of the financial return continuum thereby legitimizing all the degrees of return when giving priority to the common good. Those of us seasoned in this movement are confident that as people learn more they will naturally continue to move more in this direction. Over the recent years we have consistently witnessed this happen.

Many economic organizations have emerged over the recent years, all moving in the direction of giving priority to the common good. My friend Judy Wicks and others created BALLE (Business Alliance for Local Living Economies). It focuses on having our economic activity be as local as possible. Slow Money, Businesses for Social Responsibilty, and Social Venture Network (SVN) are a few of the others. And the cooperative movements have found new vitality.

Finally, and perhaps most important, impact investing has brought attention to the fact that all investments have social and environmental impacts to which we need to attend. Thus impact investing is also definitely a positive step forward.

Common Good Investing

The next step in the maturation of these movements will be common good investing.

This is where it is recognized that it is only possible to have one highest priority.

It is either the common good or something less than the common good, a part of the indivisible universe. The latter always results in a person giving priority to the self-interest of the only part of the universe over which he or she has sole and complete control: his or her physical body, or by extension, to something to which his or her identity is attached, such as children, family, religious congregation, a company, or a nation.

Whether or not responsible investing begins calling itself "impact investing" or "common good investing," or just changes its actions without changing the name, is not what is most important. Whatever the words to describe it might become, we will at some point in the future insist that the *highest priority* of companies be the common good and we will remain in a constant conversation on how to do it because what we agree is the common good is always maturing.

As mentioned earlier, this will result in a "common good investment movement" including the emergence of common good investment funds. They will invest in companies where the priority is the common good and they provide common good audits by creditable third parties.

In this chapter many options were presented as ways you can participate in the Common Good Capitalism Movement. It is my hope that you choose to participate in whatever large or small ways you find to be a fit for you.

Allow me to conclude this chapter by pointing out that when in the 1970s we began the "socially responsible investment movement" nearly everyone said we were crazy and it would never happen. People would continue to only do two things: 1) invest to make the most money, and 2) donate some of their profits to charitable and educational organizations. We argued that there would increasingly be more people who would like their investments to definitely not being making the world a worst place and instead be actively making it a better place.

So, as mentioned twice earlier, in the late 1970s fifteen of us met once a month for eighteen months and wrote one of the first comprehensive "social screens for investing." In 1982, Wayne Silby and I, two of the members of that group, used those screens to create the Calvert Family of Socially Responsible Mutual Funds, the first family of such funds. Basically we only invested in companies that had good relationships with their employees, the community, and the environment. We did not speak to their highest priority, the maximization of the financial return to the shareholders. However, we did invest in companies that were doing at least a minimum good job of relating well with their employees, the community, and the environment in ways that were giving priority to the common good.

As also described earlier, today socially responsible investing, now labeled "impact investing," is becoming mainstream. Why did those of us who began this movement back in the 1970s know this would eventually happen when nearly all were telling us we were naïve? We didn't have the words for it at that time. However, intuitively we knew that maturation is the fundamental process in nature, this was a more mature way of investing, and therefore it was inevitable.

As I finish this chapter I know many readers will easily assume that common good capitalism will never happen. It appears to be going against the current established order. It is not. It is a maturation of it. The future is not the past. That is why I can again confidently write, "It is inevitable."

6
Corporations

MANY ARE NOT AWARE THAT THE AMERICAN REVOLUTION
was not only against Britain but also its legal extension, the East India Company. At that time it accounted for more than half of world trade. It owned the tea on the ship that the Colonists destroyed by throwing it into the sea, later known as the Boston Tea Party that began the American Revolution. Therefore the American founders were strongly against the existence of corporations created by governments. They only knew them as extensions of an oppressive state.

It is worth remembering that the original American settlers were fleeing European dictatorships and they were spiritually devout people. Part of finding the courage to leave their homeland and loved ones, probably forever, was the making of a deep commitment to themselves to build a new way of life based on peaceful and loving relationships instead of social stratification.

A clash between the old ways and this dream became the source of an insurrection by 100 indentured servants on the first ship of Puritans to our shores, the Mayflower. The night before they were to leave the ship and step on the American shore for the first time, the indentured servants revolted. The British corporation that had financed the Puritans' voyage had claimed most of the fruits of their labors for seven years as well. The Pilgrims joined with the indentured servants against the few masters on board. The result was that all the adult males signed the Mayflower Pact in which they agreed they would all step on American soil as free men. That night they established a government in which all men (they were not yet mature enough to include women) had an equal voice and vote.

They established Plymouth Rock as the first American colony settled by Europeans; it was organized as a cooperative commonwealth. Like the American Indians who were already there, they put all the products of their labors into a common warehouse and took their needs from a common store for three years. After that, the masters who had financed the first voyage returned from England with additional forces and demanded the indentured servants' seven years of servitude. This ended the cooperative village, after which the sponsors assumed power over their indentured servants. However, they organized their village and state governments as democracies.

Cooperation for the common good continued to be the basis for the way of life of most of the new settlers who followed them. Many fulfilled the original American dream of creating a commonwealth, small cooperative townships throughout the land. When the consensus was lost, a group with common beliefs would pick up, move deeper into the wilderness, and create another cooperative village around a common piece of land called "the town common." Most towns throughout New England still circle these town commons where all used to be free to graze their livestock. A number of New England states still have the word commonwealth in their names; for example, "The Commonwealth of Massachusetts," the first state.

In the 18th and 19th centuries they described their dream as a "cooperative commonwealth." In 1800, just a few percent of free Americans worked for someone else. To do so was viewed as one tiny step above slavery, the indentured servitude that was still being offered in exchange for being brought to America. Free people were either self-employed working the land or using their hands. Today, more than 85 percent of Americans work for someone else. The story of the USA during the 1800s is one of failed efforts by Americans in the face of the Industrial Revolution to prevent the erosion of the "cooperative commonwealth" they knew in their rural townships. Neither capitalism nor socialism was their choice. By the end of the 19th century the fight had been lost and was abandoned. The dream that continually brought people to these shores had to retreat back into people's personal lives for fulfillment. The larger dream went back into the hearts of us all and silence while the battle between capitalism and socialism consumed the attention of nearly all.

In today's world common good capitalism could become the fulfillment of the original American dream, albeit in different forms then they imagined. It is based on equality, individual freedom, free markets, and voluntarily giving priority to the common good.

Yet, to continue the above story, in 1790 and when one of these rural towns in New England needed to raise money to build a bridge, they created an organization separate from the democratic town government to manage it and gave it the name "a corporation."

Imagine a piece of paper with many lines drawn down and across it so there were many little boxes. Each box was given the same financial value that was a very small amount; assume one dollar in today's money. This would allow every person in town the ability to buy at least one "share" of the loan to the town to build the bridge. Then the by-laws stated that, like the town meeting, there was one vote per shareholder, not one vote per share. Thus, this corporation operated democratically, like the town meeting. When the bridge was built there was a small toll to use it. When the loan plus interest was repaid to all, the corporation ceased to exist.

During the Spanish Civil War of 1812 this corporate model was used to create companies to produce guns, uniforms, and other products needed to fight the war. When the war ended, the companies remained in existence and switched to making products for citizens. Corporations quickly began to emerge in every state, each voted into existence by the state legislators whose members often benefited financially by being some of the first investors in them. Eventually there arose a strong grassroots movement to get rid of them, calling them "the new East India Companies."

In 1828 Andrew Jackson ran for President and was elected with one of his promises being to get rid of the corporations. Once elected, he switched his position. Instead he encouraged states to allow anyone to set up a corporation without having to receive approval by the legislators. This was accepted as an adequate keeping of his promise to end the self-serving relationship between members of state legislators and the corporations. The fact that people were at different levels of understanding how to do this was ignored.

In 1890 a New York law student took a ferry to New Jersey and convinced its Governor that he could easily be re-elected by declaring that he would end the state income tax. He could do this by changing its corporate laws to allow limited liability and existence in perpetuity. The result would be that corporations throughout America would switch to be incorporated in New Jersey and their fees to do so would end the need for the state income tax. He was re-elected on this platform and did this. Every other state eventually followed with the same policies.

You can learn more about this history and how the laws and courts ended up creating the set of corporate for-profit and non-profit laws we have today by reading John Curl's book *The History of Work Cooperation in America* and Ted Nace's book *Gangs of America: The Rise of Corporate Power and the Disabling of Democracy*. The result is that today corporations can be created by anyone in any state, they live in perpetuity, there is one vote per share, and they have limited liability which means the officers cannot be sued for the actions of the corporations unless there is fraud. Now, as a result of the 2010 *Citizens United vs. Federal Elections Commission* decision of the Supreme Court, there is no restriction on corporate, as well as individual and union, contributions to a political campaign's allied Political Action Committee (PAC) whereas individual contributions to a candidate are capped at $2,700.

It can easily be argued that it is good for society for people's total personal assets to not be at risk when they invest some of them in a corporation to produce a product or service for the good of society: limited liability. It can also be easily argued that it is good for society for companies to not have to go out of business after a certain number of years: to legally live in perpetuity.

However in 1818 a judge settled a case by creating two kinds of corporations, for-profit and non-profit corporations. In setting this pattern in motion he legalized the *priority* of a for-profit corporation to be the financial interests of the shareholders and the *priority* of a non-profit corporation to be any activity for the good of society. Still living within the immature assumption that separate parts are real, this judge *inadvertently* legitimized the priority of the for-profit company being *something other than the common good of society*. Thus, it was eventually easily concluded by many, especially since the 1970s and the emergence of the philosophy of the economist Milton Freidman, that the for-profit company was exempt from the fundamental priority of all members and groups in a society. Its *priority* is the financial interests of the shareholders and it is the priority of governments and non-profits to act for the common good, not them.

Thus today for-profit corporations often behave as if they have a legal exemption from this most fundamental agreement we all make with one another when we agree to be members of a society.

As the above books document, this immature worldview has been sustained and built upon by similar immature thinking ever since. However we are now ready to move beyond it and, thankfully, there is still nothing legally preventing companies from reaching agreements that give priority to the common good.

Today it is important for readers to know how large and powerful a small number of corporations have become.

All of the following quotes will be from a white paper recently commissioned by Calvert Investments and available on its website, www.calvert. com. Its title is *The Role of the Corporation in Society: Implications for Investors*. The lead author is George Serafeim, Jakurski Family Associate Professor of Business Administration at the Harvard Business School. Joining him in its preparation is Emily Kaiser, Esq., Josh Linder, Kim Nguyen-Taylor, Ivan Naranjo, CFA, FRM, and John Streur all from Calvert Investments. Here are some of the first words in the document:

The 500 largest companies in the world comprise approximately 50% of the world's stock market capitalization. This is an astonishing statistic considering that there are close to 50,000 unique publicly listed and actively traded companies around the world...Over time, companies have accumulated increased power relative to other stakeholders. This power has given corporations a license not only to operate, but also to grow and reach a wide diversity of stakeholders across geographies. The largest 500 corporations in the world directly employed more than 43 million people, indirectly controlled hundreds of millions of workers in their supply chain, paid more than $700 billion in taxes, sold products and services worth over $22 trillion, controlled assets valued at more than $100 trillion, and in 2014 spent more than $1.6 trillion and $400 billion in capital and research and development expenditures, respectively. The higher financial, human, and technological capabilities of companies compared with the limitations of governments due to indebtedness, inability to attract human capital, and the lack of jurisdiction in a global marketplace uniquely position corporations to respond to environmental and social challenges.

The following evidences the power in the marketplace of some of our multinational corporations:

...Google's Gmail product serves approximately 900 million people, more than the population of Europe. The Goggle search engine's 5-minute service lapse in August 2013 caused global Internet traffic to drop by 40%...Walmart hosts more than 250 million customers in its stores each week and approximately 80% of all U. S. consumers at some point during a typical year. The company uses approximately 0.5% of all electricity produced in the United States, ranking it ahead of 12 states in electricity consumption.

It can also be pointed out that Facebook has over 1.6 billion members, is continuing to grow at a rapid pace, and where it operates it has a virtual monopoly in its product market.

As for-profit corporations have grown in size and scale their negative impact upon society is significant: environmental degradation, a decline in air and water quality, and water pollution. For instance, commercial agriculture is causing more than half of the deforestation and in 2013 the combined activities of agricultural and industrial companies accounted for approximately 88% of worldwide fresh water withdrawals. To sustain growth they continue to need vast amounts of human and natural capital.

In addition we are now clearly a global village. "The Apple iPod illustrates the type of consumer product that could only exist in such an interconnected world market. The iPod contains 451 distinct components, the ten most valuable of which originate in six different countries."

It is clear that in this "new global village society" we need the leaders of our multinational corporations to mature to where they understand that at full human maturity in the skill of self-consciousness their highest priority is the common good and, thus, the priority of their companies as well.

It is also clear that some of them are on the boards of companies that are very profitable often as a result of their duopoly monopoly positions:

The scale and global footprint of corporations reinforces the moral argument for corporate action...This vast concentration in economic activity and the associated power relative to consumers, suppliers, and smaller competitors is reflected in the higher profitability margins that these companies earn. Specifically, in 2014, the combined return-on-assets of the largest 500 companies was almost double that of all other publicly listed firms (4.7% versus 2.5%).

Eventually public pressure, in combination with the maturation in the skill of self-consciousness of our corporate leaders, will force them into voluntarily reaching agreements with their duopoly partners that give priority to the common good. Otherwise our hope can be that they do so because it will increase the profitability of their company:

> ...a company's purpose and contribution to society can also lead to higher employee engagement...Studies have found positive relationships between employee engagement and organizational performance outcomes including employee retention, productivity, profitability, customer loyalty, and safety. In terms of profitability, research has shown that companies with more engaged employees are likely to exceed the industry average in revenue growth.

We are happy to welcome corporate leaders into our common good corporate community whether because of maturation in the skill of self-consciousness or because they believe it will increase profitability. The reason is that we know maturation is the fundamental process in nature and they will be unable to avoid learning about it and embracing it as a result of being in the presence of those who have matured into full freedom.

Corporations survive and thrive by responding to the maturation in the thinking of the public. As we mature into full freedom they will respond to it. Currently they are responding to the public's increasing awareness of our human effects upon the environment:

> In interviews conducted in 69 countries for PricewaterhouseCoopers (PwC) 14th Annual Global CEO Survey, almost half of the CEOs expected consumers to factor environmental and corporate responsibility practices into purchasing decisions. The CEOs indicated that they would adjust their strategy in the next three years to capture this consumer and employee sentiment.

Today costumers clearly prefer doing business with companies that are perceived as caring in some ways about the common good. In doing so these companies also benefit financially. After providing statistical evidence, *The Role of the Corporation in Society* concludes, "Considerable evidence indicates that firms with sustainable business practices face lower capital constraints."

Maturation is the fundamental process in nature and it cannot be stopped, only delayed. The maturation of more of us each year into the higher layers of maturity in the skill of self-consciousness will eventually result in the voluntary creation in the private sector of common good capitalism.

Here is the result of a survey that suggests we may be further in this direction than many of us may know:

> Consider, for example, surveys that show that more than 80% of the citizens in countries including the United States, United Kingdom, Germany, France, Canada, and Japan agree with the statement that, "Corporations should create economic value in a way that aligns with society's interests, even if that means sacrificing shareholder returns."

The black swan phenomenon is when something fully unexpected happens and has a major effect, such as a black swan being born when we were assuming all swans are white. For many on both the political left and right it cannot be imagined that common good capitalism will emerge. As far as anyone can remember it has never happened in the past. Indeed, it will be fully unexpected by most. However maturation is the fundamental process in nature. Therefore when it emerges it may be a surprise to many; but it will eventually emerge. The future is never the past.

It will then become the dominant economic process on Earth just as democracy is continuing to become the dominant form of government on Earth.

Adam Smith, Karl Marx, Thomas Piketty, and Common Good Capitalism

Adam Smith, the eighteenth century author of *The Wealth of Nations*, thought he had found a way out of a system of inequality with the competitive free market economy because of its ability to create ample wealth.

He then assumed a moral government would make sure the wealth was fairly distributed. He was right about the first part but wrong about the second part. He did not understand the progressive nature of the layers of maturity of the skill of self-consciousness. Therefore, he failed to notice that people still operating as if one of the lower layers of maturity of this skill is the highest layer, the Baby to Adult Layers, would naturally give priority to their self-interest, not the common good, and structure a government to support it.

Karl Marx, the author in 1848 of *The Communist Manifesto,* set out to solve this problem; but he also failed for the same reason. In particular, he did not know of the existence of the Elder Layer where people mature to where they have the skill of freely choosing to give priority to the common good. Therefore, he saw the solution involving the working class overthrowing the ruling class. This also explains why he wrote extensively about the short-comings of capitalism but not how business life would be conducted in a communist society.

In 2013, Thomas Piketty, the author of *Capital in the Twenty-first Century,* produced solid data to substantiate what Marx had seen. Piketty: "A free market continuously creates inequality." He continues, "Therefore, there is no natural, spontaneous process to prevent destabilizing, inegalitarian forces from prevailing permanently." He also discovered that this pattern has existed throughout history: "...in all known societies in all times, the least wealthy half of the population has owned virtually nothing," and the top ten per cent has owned "most of what there is to own." Here we are not talking about tribal societies but all of the others.

Piketty's lengthy book provides the data that reveals that to this day this inequality continues because no one has found the solution and implemented it. (Menand, Louis, "He's Back," *The New Yorker,* October 10, 2016, p. 90.)

Common good capitalism solves this ancient problem.

Its key ingredient is that it understands and honors the existence of layers of maturity of the skill of self-consciousness. It then provides a way to solve it that not only honors the Baby to Adult Layers but also the Elder

Layer, the layer many on Earth are now discovering and mastering as a skill. For them it will be a natural, effortless, and a joyful free choice to give priority to the common good. Secondly, they can imagine a solution that doesn't compromise away the obvious creativity and wealth production of competitive free markets. It is to have the competitors in each product market freely choose to meet and reach agreements that give priority to the common good, not just of the owners and employees but of us all. It is similar to the way the productive area guilds operated in a much earlier time. Then for them and the public to trust that all the competitors are keeping the agreements, and also so the public will have input into their continuous agreement making process, all competitors will provide annual common good as well as financial audits to the public.

This is an honoring of the Elder Layer of maturity as the solution.

As mentioned earlier, it is not possible to police each person to be sure each moment he or she is giving priority to the common good, our most fundamental agreement with each other in a society. This can only be the result of free choice. Therefore, it will only be experienced as natural, effortless, and enjoyable to do it if it is experienced as the next higher layer of maturity in the skill of self-consciousness.

Adam Smith, Karl Marx, and Thomas Piketty, and all the others who have done a great job of analyzing the problem were unable to provide the design of a solution because they did not know the practical way to integrate the third dimension of self-consciousness (oneness) into their proposed solutions. And they couldn't have discovered the importance of this without understanding the relationship between human languages and the oneness of nature so they stopped unconsciously projecting the assumption that separate parts are real into their designs. Therefore, the possibility that together the owners and the employees would become capable of freely choosing to give priority to the common good in a way all in society would enthusiastically support and participate was unable to be imagined. This is now easily possible because of the emergence of the Information Age.

Common good capitalism is inevitable for one reason. Those who do understand the existence of the seven layers of maturity of the skill of self-consciousness as the practical way to integrate the oneness of nature into their daily lives will not be able to stop themselves from doing it. Maturation is the fundamental process of nature.

Thank you Adam Smith, Karl Marx, and Thomas Piketty, you among many others have helped us get here.

7

Some of Us are Ready to Mature Ourselves and Our Societies into the Elder and Mature Elder Layers

IN THE 1600s SOME OF US HAD MATURED INTO THE TEEN LAYER of maturity in the skill of self-consciousness and were ready to organize our societies based on it. Those were the Pilgrims who had journeyed to the American lands partially so they could do it, forming the United States of America. It became the first democratic society that has been sustained. As mentioned earlier, today two-thirds of the nations on Earth are democracies. This global maturation of us as individuals and societies into the Teen Layer has continued but is still far from being a *universally known knowledge skill*, like the knowledge skill of a human language and agreeing the Earth is round.

Since then more and more people have been living at the Adult Layer. This is where their highest priority becomes their freely chosen outside belief. In the USA, for instance, our major political arguments occur between the differing fundamental outside belief of the Republicans and Democrats. Most other nations are also divided into two or more major political parties, each with a slightly different fundamental outside belief that is honored by all subsequent beliefs they hold.

Giving priority to our outside beliefs, regardless of their content, is operating as individuals and societies at the Adult Layer of the skill of self-consciousness. It is still giving our power to a second thing only now it is a second thing in the separate parts of our thinking rather than outside our physical bodies. It is giving our power to an outside belief. Thus at all times it is necessary to check if our behavior is honoring this second player: our voluntary outside belief. If it is present we are not free to respond to the particular situation in front of us in the exact appropriate way. We first give priority to *obeying* the outside belief.

Many people are now ready to mature into the Elder and Mature Elder

Layers. Just as the maturation of some people and their societies into each lower layer of maturity changed the fundamental container of everything in their thinking, this will change everything in their fundamental way of thinking as well.

The most fundamental change will be from giving one's power to a second thing in one's thinking, an outside belief, to not giving it to a second thing anymore, full freedom.

These people will understand the importance of keeping their power. They now know that from the inside no one else can think their thoughts or move their arms and legs.

Therefore to be free to respond *exactly appropriately* in each particular situation, they need to have their power, all of it.

They now know that the only way to keep their power is to be a personal scientist, to primarily go to their immediate direct experience to identify their accurate fundamental truth. This is the *only way* to keep their power, all of it, and have it fully available each moment in the future.

When they do this they eventually discover that the universe is an indivisible whole because in language this is the accurate way to represent what they are always immediately and directly experiencing as self-evident: everything is connected to everything else, mutually interdependent, and equally real.

If this is, indeed, the accurate fundamental belief about reality, all will eventually discover it to be true in their direct experience. This has it primarily be a knowledge skill and secondly be an inside belief in a language.

Now, for people who have grown into Elders, there is no outside authority to obey. Now they can confirm that this is the accurate fundamental fact in any moment by simply turning their attention to witnessing that this is true. As a result they have kept their power, all of it, and are now personal scientists, fully free human beings.

The result, of course, is to notice that they have a *new fundamental inside belief,* what we earlier described as an inside belief because it is now second in priority in their thinking to their direct experience of its accuracy. It is no longer "I am a separate part in competition with all other parts of the universe with my priority being the self-interest of my physical body." Instead it is "The universe is an indivisible whole, I am part of it, and my true primary and mature self-interest is the continuous maturation of my total self, the universe."

It is eventually noticed that they also have a *new self-definition*. Instead of defining "self" as "my physical body" they now define it as "I am first the universe that will not die and second my physical body that will die."

Elders also eventually realize they are always primarily using the pattern of thinking that does not assume separate parts (time and space) are real. *While fully doing both, they now give priority to the oneness pattern of thinking.* They give priority to priorities in their thinking and second priority to this or that in time and space.

They begin mastering the skill of doing both simultaneously because they know they are equally valuable. The latter is the skill that allows them to be self-conscious and the former accurately represents reality in the pattern of their thinking.

They also know exactly what will be their priority each moment in the future: *whatever each judges from the spot where each is standing to be the best unique action for the maturation of the universe.* Herein we are labeling this *activity* what it has been most often labeled throughout history: eldering. This *behavior* has most often been labeled moral behavior. It is "freely choosing to give priority to the common good."

This knowledge provides a much higher and consistent experience of inner peace than they have known before. They also realize that they have intuitively known inner peace as their birthright while maturing up the layers of maturity of the skill of self-consciousness. The oneness of nature and its partner, thinking pain, were continuously pushing and pulling them up the layers of the skill of self-consciousness.

This was the fundamental process of maturation in nature moving in them.

They are now aware that they knew it non-self-consciously as a baby and toddler and that what has been primarily going on is that they have been mastering the skill of knowing it *while also being self-conscious.* This personal inner experience of peace, of fundamental happiness, as the container within which everything else is occurring in their thinking and perceptions is more enjoyable than giving their power to a second thing, herein called an "outside belief." So they cannot resist fully, naturally, and effortlessly embracing the highest and final layer of maturity in the skill, the Mature Elder Layer. This is where they give priority to the experience of this truth rather than the words representing it.

With a bit of a chuckle they realize that this joy of the fundamental experience of happiness was not the result of seeking personal happiness. It was the result of discovering the accurate definition of "self."

Now they cannot resist always giving priority to the common good! It is where the greatest personal joy of happiness is self-consciously experienced.

These people will not be able to stop themselves from maturing capitalism business into common good business. The days of solving problems by *primarily* creating two or more teams and forcing them to fight, including getting around the rules, changing them without having the priority be the common good, and cheating if they can find a way to get away with it, are over. They will take full responsibility for making sure their organizations, for-profit or non-profit, are always giving priority to the common good as best they can. They will also voluntarily cooperate with the "other team or teams in their freely chosen league" to do this in every way they can. They will still enjoy competition as a secondary form of cooperation because it honors individual freedom, free markets, creativity, and maturation. It allows anyone to come up with a better idea. However they will aggressively create a safe space within which it occurs so no one can easily get hurt.

Trusts for All Children

No child should be born and mature in poverty.

My friend Paul Polak, with Mel Warwick the authors of *A Business Solution to Poverty,* is the creator of affordable services for the poorest of the poor on a for-profit basis so the services continue to be provided. Each year he makes it a discipline to interview more than 100 poor people. He has consistently told me that basically they all end up, in one way or another, saying the same thing: "we need more money.

A long time ago we all lived in villages where all chipped in as best they could and all had enough food, clothing, shelter, medical care, and time to raise their children well, initiate them at appropriate times, and enjoy singing, dancing, and playing in community.

Then someone invented money.

Now some people could focus on accumulating money. Those who were successful thought they no longer needed the village. They could buy all they needed and wanted. Those who instead focused on having fun with friends, falling in love, raising children, philosophy, scholarship, the arts, and science eventually discovered they needed to get enough money to acquire the food, clothing, shelter, etc. that they and their children needed. Since those who learned how to make money saw it as only wise to use it to make more money, while only donating some of it to charities, it was not easy for the others to make enough money.

Worse, since to survive all were now on their own seeking enough money, the most widespread disease became loneliness and the lack of the experience of meaning in their lives. This was largely a result of no longer being in mutually supportive communities. In some places this disease became known as "emotional depression."

We are now coming to understand how this occurred and how to use money in a way that reverses this social disease. As a result there are three things we will eventually mature into doing. They will begin to end the widespread diseases of loneliness, depression, and an absence of meaning:

1. **Permanently Ending Poverty.** No one chooses to be in poverty. Therefore like before money we must provide all who need it adequate food, clothing, shelter, etc. to remain above extreme poverty by monthly distributions to them of enough money with no strings attached so they can maintain their dignity. Money resulted in Earth having nearly half of the people living in poverty so money also needs to be used to end it. All will then surely contribute to the welfare of us all as best as they can, hopefully, in addition to finding a fulfilling job, by primarily learning

how to elder themselves and their children up the layers to full maturity in the skill of self-consciousness. Then the latter will be the highest priority in our societies rather than survival by acquiring enough money.

2. **Re-Villaging Our Lives.** We must all become aware of the layers of maturity of being a human being—the layers of maturity of the skill of self-consciousness—and re-village our lives in a modern context so we can more easily and enjoyably elder each other. Within it will emerge many respected and skilled elders capable of assisting the rest of us, and especially the children, up the layers to full human maturity in the skill of self-consciousness. Only re-villaging for this purpose can end the loneliness, depression, and lack of meaning experienced by many.

3. **Common Good Capitalism.** We must establish a movement where, while fully doing both, the voluntary highest priority of all moneymaking activities is the common good and profit is the second priority, primarily to be able to continue providing their products or services.

Trusts for All Children, Inc., a 501c3 charitable and educational organization we have created, is designed to do the first by creating in the private sector a forever growing fund where the annual profits will be distributed to poor families so they remain above extreme poverty. It will be described below. The re-villaging of our lives will be briefly described later. And the focus of this book is the creation of the option of a common good capitalism economic sector.

It is also clear that artificial intelligence and automation will result in fewer jobs. In addition people will live longer. All three are good things if all of our children's families have a monthly income to remain above extreme poverty. *More important they will be able to focus more on maturation than on survival that is most important for the health and happiness of us all.*

The human species will be continually maturing. Thus at some point in the future the fear of poverty to motivate people to seek a job will become history because we will not allow anyone to live in poverty. So the question arises, "Rather than waiting for all governments to adequately do this how could we set something in motion in the private sector that all would trust will ultimately accomplish it and, importantly, without the possibility of budget cuts as a result of the swings of the political pendulums?"

There are two basic ways to acquire money: 1) be paid a salary for work, or 2) not work, own stock and other assets and collect dividends, interest, or rents. Wealthy people do not work and have income primarily as a result of owning stocks. *Thus what we want to do is find a way to have stock market profits provide the income necessary for all families on Earth to remain above extreme poverty. This would be a private sector solution to poverty.* It would be creating a trust for all poor people in the same way wealthy families create a trust for each of their children. And it would be providing the main thing poor people need in a monetary economy: more money

Here is our current design of how Trusts for All Children (TAC) will work. As were our first designs, it is not a harnessing of self-interest to accomplish it (calling on our primary motivation at the lower five layers of maturity). It is a harnessing of our deep intuitive care for each other as members of our now global village (calling on our access to the higher two layers). It will, therefore, be an experiment to see if such an invitation can be successful at this point in our mutual maturation.

Anyone can become a member of TAC by monthly donating $1 by electronic transfer ($12 a year). This way only one decision needs to be made and it will continue until it is stopped. This money will be used to cover TAC's operating expenses. At this price nearly everyone can join. *Also, this way every person who joins is an equal owner of the mission of TAC.*

Then each member, if he or she so chooses and guided by his or her ability and desire to participate, can add to their monthly donation to TAC as much additional capital as they choose: $5 so the total is $6, $10 so the total is $11, $50 so the total is $51, $100 so the total is $101, or $1,000 so the total is $1,001. *100% of any addition to their membership fee will go into the "trust for poor children."* Of course members can at anytime raise or lower the monthly amount. At anytime they can also make additional one-time donations to the trust for poor children. These donations will be fully tax-deductible. This means that in the US the government will be covering a percentage of these contributions based on one's annual tax bracket (between 0 and 39%).

The capital in the "trust for poor children" will primarily be invested in responsible or common good index funds. As mentioned earlier, for more than 23 years they have performed as well as the S&P 500 Index that is a diversified group of the five hundred largest US companies. Responsible companies have good relationships with their employees, the community, and the environment. The funds will primarily be invested in common good indices.

Each year the net profit will be distributed to families to keep them above extreme poverty. In years where there is a loss, some of the capital in the trust will be used to maintain the same level of distributions as the previous year. Thus, since additional money is being received monthly, the performance of the stock market will only sustain or speed up the distributions but never stop them. Over the last 86 years, including both the Great Depression of 1929 and Great Recession of 2008, the US stock market has had an average annual return of more than 10%.

Therefore, the capital in the trust for poor children will be forever using the profits of responsible companies toward eventually putting a permanent end to extreme poverty on Earth. Instead of raising $100,000, giving it to poor people and gone, it will be invested and the average of $10,000 profit each year will be donated annually forever to be sure we eventually bring an end to poverty on earth.

There is a second purpose of TAC. It is to also create a trust for every child.

99% of families believe they cannot easily create a trust for each of their children. Therefore this is a virgin market. They also do not know that if over the last 60 years they had put $10 a month into the equivalent of the S&P 500 Index it would today be $1 million. So TAC will educate families how they can use small monthly electronic transfers by family members and friends to create a trust for each of their children or grandchildren that could provide them a forever growing larger monthly income and, when elderly, the equivalent of a monthly US Social Security check.

A serious of options on how they can do this will be presented. They will be easy to understand and inexpensive. There will be options offered by TAC where the capital will grow without taxation, which means that usually each year there would be more assets in the trust. Therefore, the monthly distributions will usually be larger each year. In exchange for the absence of taxation the balance upon the death of the child would remain with TAC and added to the trust for poor children. TAC will also introduce members to a number of asset management organizations, such as Calvert Funds, Stakeholders Capital,

Pax World Funds, and Parnassus Funds, where they can create responsible trusts for their children with low fees. Here their children's children can inherit the balance upon their death. Finally, they will also assist them in creating college savings plans and government sponsored retirement funds that provide tax benefits.

Thus, the second goal of TAC is to be the one stop shop to create inexpensive trusts for all children that are easily grown through monthly contributions from family members and friends.

For instance, if ten family members and friends (mom, dad, both sets of grandparents, and two Godmothers and two Godfathers) commit to donate $10 a month ($120 a year each) for 20 years, the child beginning at 18 years old will receive each quarter a small but nearly always larger distribution to remain above extreme poverty. And when elderly, he or she will receive the equivalent of a US Social Security check until death. In addition, if members in wealthier communities and nations assist parents in poorer communities around the world to create a trust fund for each of their children, eventually every child on Earth can be born with a trust fund fueled by the profits from our responsible corporations.

Finally, extremely wealthy people can now easily participate in bringing about a permanent end to extreme poverty. They simply need to write a check to TAC's trust for poor children. *It will forever provide distributions to the families of poor children.* Warren Buffett and Melinda and Bill Gates have created an association of billionaires—now with over 100 members—who have committed to donating 50% of their wealth to charity before they die. We hope they find TAC to be an attractive option. Also, TAC will create robust fundraising programs to add additional capital to the fund. In addition, states can compete to be the first ones to end extreme poverty in their states. They can grow the membership in their state with the members committing to have their donations first used to end extreme poverty in their state. Donors can also designate certain nations for the use of their capital, such as South Sudan or Bangledesh. Through responsible organizations, such as the Campaign for Human Development (CHD) that has offices in 150 nations, and the major microloan programs around the world, such as the Grameen Bank, the capital can be distributed monthly to poor families, even if it is necessary to do it using cash.

What is determined to be a poor family or person and the appropriate amount to keep the family or person above extreme poverty is a process that will have to be designed and continuously monitored. However this is a small task to demand of ourselves in the interest of accomplishing this responsibility we all have to our fellow human beings on Earth now that we live in a monetary world and a global village. It is 2016, not 1016. It is time we created in the private sector the equivalent of a trust fund for every poor child on Earth and one for every non-poor child as well.

In doing so we will have created a safe place for families to give priority to maturation rather than survival.

As Elder and Mature Elder Layer participants in our now global village, ending extreme poverty is our primary collective responsibility for the common good, for the safety of all. So we will want to attend to programs like this and attend to them quickly and fully.

We are currently looking for a CEO and funding to launch TAC. If interested give me a call: Terry Mollner, 413-563-3700.

By the way, there may be something more important that Trusts for All Children can accomplish than setting in motion something that will eventually provide a monthly income to every poor and non-poor child on Earth to remain above extreme poverty:

Once up and growing it can provide the evidence that we can work together as individuals in the private sector, as an actual global village of people, toward eventually bringing about an end to something as important as ending extreme poverty on Earth. It will be the behavior of first being citizens of the universe and secondly citizens of a nation on Earth.

Common Good Behavior Cannot be Legislated

Allow me to mention here that, like Trusts for All Children, all of these maturations into the Elder and Mature Layers social order will primarily occur in the private sector.

Moral behavior cannot be legislated.

It is not possible to create a policy and police it in a way that obligates each person to at all times give priority to the best unique action for the common good. The primary purpose of our geographically defined nations will become perceived as creating a safe space, a private sector, where people can freely choose to associate to build the common good society.

Moral behavior, mature behavior, can only be the result of the free choice each moment of individuals.

Therefore it must be voluntary. Anyone can join or leave any for-profit or non-profit organization in the private sector of a nation. Thus organizations within the private sector honor full freedom.

A person cannot easily leave one's geographically defined nation. Thus, people often experience themselves as not supported at being fully free as citizens of our geographically defined nations. However they always experience themselves as fully free when, in the private sector, they can easily join or leave an organization.

We Can Only Freely Choose to Give Priority to the Common Good

I mentioned earlier that I attended the first Conscious Capitalism Conference in Austin, Texas organized by John Mackey, the founder and now Co-CEO of Whole Foods, Inc. At dinner on Saturday evening I was sitting at a table of about seven people with John being one of them. A person, in speaking with John, referred to him as a libertarian. John interrupted the person and said, "I am an *integral* libertarian!"

The person was a bit stunned and then asked, "What is an integral libertarian?" John spoke for well over five minutes trying to explain what it was and how it differed from regular libertarianism.

I listened intently. I knew his highest priority was individual freedom, the essence of libertarianism. However I also knew he was a devout student of a wonderful set of spiritual books called *A Course In Miracles*. So I knew he cared about the common good. What he was clearly struggling with over the five minutes he was speaking was how to unite those two while unconsciously speaking within the assumption that separate parts are real. He did not know how to integrate in the third dimension of the skill of self-consciousness, the oneness of nature, represented in language by giving priority to priorities. He was only using the first two dimensions of the skill of self-consciousness, the *recognition of differences* and the use of the *mutual illusion tool of time and space (the separate parts of languages)*.

So when he was done I spoke: "John, I think I could state what you said in one sentence." He slouched down in his chair and shook his head in a way that clearly revealed that he definitely did not think that was possible. I continued.

"Your highest priority," I said, "is individual freedom. But when a person reaches the higher layers of maturity he or she freely chooses to give priority to the common good."

Like a rocket he catapulted from his chair and threw half of his body and extended arm and index finger fully across the table toward me and shouted, "That's it!"

What I had done was honor his fundamental belief as legitimate. Then I brought in the third dimension of the skill of self-consciousness, the oneness of nature, as the container of it by including the existence of layers of maturity (prioritization). This allowed me to identify, as the result of free choice, a different highest priority when operating at a higher layer of maturity in the skill of self-consciousness.

So free choice was fully sustained but the oneness of nature was the new context. This allowed, at a higher layer of maturity, the common good to then be the new freely chosen highest priority.

He did not understand that this was what I was doing; however he, like all of us, fully knew how to think in the pattern of priorities and easily did so. By including it he was able to see the mature relationship between individual freedom and the common good. It is the giving of priority to the latter in a way that sustains the former by including the way the oneness of nature is represented in language, as layers of maturity in the skill of self-consciousness.

This is how people both on the political right and left will come to embrace this maturation into the Elder and Mature Elder Layers and, as a result, common good business.

By adding this third dimension of the skill of self-consciousness they will see that our ability and right of individual freedom is fully sustained but the free choice of our highest priority will mature to genuinely be the common good. This is the natural and effortless result of the maturation of our self-definition.

And it will be understood that shifting priority to the highest good in no way limits our ability and right of full freedom of choice. Instead it enhances our freedom by both reducing potential enemies and enabling us to also experience the joy of moving in a way that works for everyone as much as for ourselves.

Nations Defined by Agreement

Eventually this will also result in the emergence in the private sector of *nations defined by agreement* rather than geography.

Nations defined by agreement will be celebrated and greatly valued by the geographically defined nations because they will only attend to things not being done well or at all by the geographically defined nations. Basically, they will operate as non-profit organizations that will take on the responsibility of being a nation for the people who join them. So just as people are currently members of the governing body of their town, state, and nation, and of for-profit and non-profit organizations, they will also be members of the governing body of their nation defined by agreement.

They will emerge because people will no longer be willing to wait to get something done they judge to be wise until those who strongly disagree with them join in a majority vote. Or do something in the direction of it and not well designed as a result of the necessary compromises.

Although some interests clearly have more power than others, majority vote is the assumed fundamental way decisions are made in our geographically defined democratic nations. The people who mature into the Elder Layer will conclude that they want to create in the private sector a nation of like-thinking people.

There will probably not be taxation, but rather activities paid for by fees or donations. The governing process will also primarily be a policy body based on consensus building over time, as described below.

These nations, defined by agreement rather than geography, will allow people anywhere in the world who share their worldview to join or leave it at any time. *So it will be firmly established on full freedom.* Its task will be to give priority to the common good in such a beautiful way that people will want to join and remain members.

What is begun and successful by these nations defined by agreement will eventually also be supported by geographically defined nations. For instance, Louis O. Kelso piloted the idea of employee stock ownership by all employees in companies. When it was proven to be successful for both the employees as well as the company's productivity, people learned about it. When in the 1980s Senator Russell Long of Louisiana, then the Chair of the Senate Finance Committee, learned about it he appointed Jeff Gates to be the lead staff person of the committee and create and pass legislation that provided tax benefits to owners who provided shares to their employees. They eventually got two sets of Employee Stock Ownership Plans (ESOPs) legislation passed and today millions of employees share in the financial benefits of their work beyond their salaries, not only in the USA but around the world where this legislation has been copied.

To reveal how one stimulus at the right time and in the right place can have a significant effect, in 1982 Senator Russell Long of Louisiana, the Democratic Chairman of the Senate Finance Committee, attended my Mondragon Cooperatives presentation and slide show at the invitation of the Reagan White House.

I had to take a long walk back and forth on my deck to decide if I should accept the invitation. I would be criticized for doing so by all on the political left in my cooperative employee ownership consulting community. I ultimately decided I should go because my primary responsibility was to help each person take their next step in a more mature direction.

Senator Russell Long asked questions until 1am when just a few of us were left.

He then turned to John McLaughrey, the person from the White House who had invited us, and said: "If you can get your boy to go along with this, I will be right behind him", referring to President Ronald Reagan.

The next day Jeff Gates, his chief counsel, called me. He told me that on the way home in the car Senator Long told him he was no longer his chief counsel. He was now the Head of the Staff of the Senate Finance Committee. His new job was to write and get passed what became known as Employee Stock Ownership Plans (ESOPs). The two of them got two sets of this legislation passed during the rest of the 1980s and today millions of workers participate in the ownership of the companies in which they work. It has also been copied by nations around the world.

Like the above, maturation movements usually begin in the private sector. When they have proven their value, a majority will support them. Then legislation to support them can be passed by the geographically defined nation. Therefore, one of the agendas of nations by agreement will be to build maturation movements.

Nations defined by agreement can also be used to resolve what appear to be unsolvable conflicts, such as the Israeli-Palestinian conflict. They both claim the same land as their rightful homeland. By primarily defining their nations by agreement instead of geography, they can both use the same land, the territory between the Mediterranean Sea and the Jordan River. They can each have their government and other legal structures and enact whatever laws they choose to meet their social needs. The joint management of the land can be treated like a utility district. We manage utility districts; they do not define us. Our agreements define us. So they can give their agreements priority.

All of our for-profit and non-profit organizations are primarily defined by agreement and then they may buy and use the particular parcels of land where they need them. Nations could do the same. If we became primarily nations defined by agreement, the members of the nations could be scattered around the world. It would then be more difficult to have wars over the boundaries of geographic territory when some of your citizens are living on all of the pieces of land. Therefore, this reduction of giving priority to geographically defined nation states would be a good thing.

This "priority solution" can also be used to solve many other conflicts, such as the one between the Shiites and Sunnis in the Middle East.

Common Good Parallel Democracy

Why should we primarily elect a person to office and then hope he or she supports our positions on issues? Instead, we will see that we can now create a "common good parallel democracy" in each location a democratic government (or other government) exists and directly reach agreement as a community on important issues.

Then we can have a serious and well-organized discussion of each issue and build toward a near consensus policy position.

For instance, the biggest town near my residence is Amherst, Massachusetts. We could create a non-profit organization called "Amherst Common Good Democracy (ACGD)." Then all the for-profit and non-profit organizations that choose to participate would be invited to choose their most mature statesperson to serve on the ACGD Committee. Whatever they agree is an important policy issue to consider, they will consider. It could be everything from a woman's right to an abortion or people's right to have easy access to voting to how the dozens of motorcyclists that come to town each Friday night should be handled.

If an issue position receives a 40% support of the body, it can be discussed again in that month the following year. During the year, all who want to argue for or against that position can prepare their arguments. The next year a well-organized discussion of the issue will occur and a resolution may receive a 53% vote in support. The next year, 63%. Until it or a similar proposal has received a 70% vote in support by the committee members, the decision making process on a policy is not considered complete.

The result will be that the community will become involved in a direct discussion of each issue, with the discussions able to be watched on local television channels. Second, people will have ample time to prepare their arguments for or against the proposition. Third, until there is a 70% vote in support of a position on an issue, the annual discussion continues. And, finally and most important, no one would be able to easily run for office and succeed if not in support of the policy positions taken by the ACGD.

Thus, without having any legal power, the ACGD would have the greatest power in the community. And it would be the result of a direct discussion and decisions on important policy issues by the community.

This is not a new idea. Mahatma Gandhi was the first to come up with it and one of his followers, Jayaprakash Narayan (JP), in the 1960s and 70s successfully organized it in villages all over India. However in 1976, when Indira Gandhi (no relationship) called for parliamentary elections in just six weeks in the hope of receiving a mandate to govern, it became used as a political party in cooperation with other smaller political parties to respond to her challenge. They together put up only one candidate against each of Indira Gandhi's candidates and defeated her. JP became heralded as the Second Father of India and chose Morarji Desai as the next prime minister.

A few years later, on his deathbed, JP stated that it had been a mistake to allow the Peoples Committees, as they were called, to be used to win that election. Everyone became so excited about being in the ruling political party that they abandoned the Peoples Committee system.

It was based on cooperation, maturation, and taking time to build toward a consensus on issues instead of choosing from the candidates who choose to run in a ballot box war. In villages the only people not allowed on the Peoples Committees were people involved with electoral politics. They clearly had a different highest priority, getting their person elected.

Gandhi and JP also believed that when a person, sitting in a circle and looking others in the eyes, spoke truth it would be difficult for the others to not honor it as such. They would be mutually experiencing the fundamental feeling of happiness, as when the first word was agreed upon to create a human language, which is also the experience of agreement. This would make it much easier for people to naturally and effortlessly yield to it.

At some point in the future I fully expect the re-emergence of consensus building on issues over time common good parallel democracies.

Re-Villaging of Our Lives

We will also want to re-village our lives in our modern context to create a safe place to mature our children to full maturity in the skill of self-consciousness before they enter their twenties. We will also do it to have more fun with each other that is often far more enjoyable than, for instance, sharing being an audience. This will be the result of friends joining to do this based on some common agreements. This will also become the main place people support each other in their individual maturation process, master parenting skills including skills in the eldering of their children, have rituals to celebrate each child's maturation into each next layer of maturity in the skill of self-consciousness, play music together, and create fun parties.

As described in the last section, they will also primarily be structured as consensus building over time on policies democracies. There can be clans—small groups of friends within the villages—and associations of villages that could become a nation by agreement. There can also be a board of elders solely responsible for making sure the highest priority at all times is the common good. It can be above a board of directors and executive group that executes based on the policies using invitation instead of force.

Common Good Organization Structure

This suggests a new organization structure for common good organizations (for-profit and non-profit), one that seeks to institutionalize the giving of priority to the common good. Here is one model of how this could be done.

Instead of the primary legal body being a Board of Directors it would be a Board of Elders. The Board of Directors would be directly beneath it and the executives beneath it.

The Board of Elders has only one responsibility: to be sure the highest priority at all times and in all the organization's activities is the common good as our knowledge of it matures.

It is comprised of people who are good at doing this. The Board of Directors, as is usually the current case, is comprised of people who can do a good job of establishing operational policies for the particular kind of organization. The executives execute in alignment with the mission of the organization based on these policies.

It is the contract between the Board of Elders and Board of Directors that is new and distinctive. It has three parts:

CONTRACT BETWEEN THE BOARD OF ELDERS AND BOARD OF DIRECTORS IN A COMMON GOOD ORGANIZATION

1. The Board of Elders delegates full responsibility for running the organization to the Board of Directors,
2. The Board of Elders maintains the right to veto any decision made by the Board of Directors, and
3. The Board of Elders tries to never veto a decision made by the Board of Directors. Instead it will meet with it and guide the two bodies into an agreement that all judge is giving priority to the common good as it is maturing in the society.

Two members of the Board of Elders sit as ex-officio (without vote) members of the Board of Directors. If they conclude that a decision may not be giving priority to the common good, they recommend a meeting of the two bodies for the purpose of finding an agreement all agree is giving priority to the common good for that time in the maturation of the society. The Board of Elders will do all that it can to accomplish this so it will never have to use its veto power. At the same time the very fact that the Board of

Elders has veto power will guide the Board of Directors and executives to be watchful to always give priority to participating in the maturation of the common good. Of course, if a Board of Directors strays far from a commitment to giving priority to the common good as judged by the Board of Elders, it could be removed.

Without the institutionalization of the giving of priority to the common good it can easily get lost among the list of concerns. Therefore at some point in the future many organizations, for-profit and non-profit, will create a Board of Elders to institutionalize giving priority to the common good.

Described briefly in this chapter were just five additional examples of the many new kinds of organizations, and an organizational structure, that will be created by those who mature into the Elder and Mature Elder Layers. You can learn more about them in my last book, *The Love Skill: We Are Each Mastering the 7 Layers of Human Maturity.*

Conclusion

AFTER UNILEVER BOUGHT BEN & JERRY'S IN 2000 ITS CEO-Chairman at the time (not Paul Polman the current CEO-Chairman) came to visit us from its corporate headquarters in Britain. He first spoke to our 500 employees; then he met with the board of directors. Afterwards the board and our guest went to dinner. I sat next to him and had enjoyable conversations with him and the other board members the entire evening. After dinner, when things had settled down to a comfortable rhythm, I decided to seek his point of view on a topic that held my curiosity.

I pointed out that in my opinion it is natural for us to mature to where we freely choose to give priority to the common good of us all in all we do, as individuals and in groups. Throughout history this has been defined as "moral behavior." Immoral behavior has been defined as giving priority to anything other than the common good. He agreed with this.

I went on to say that today corporations assume they are sanctioned by the state to give priority to the financial interests of the shareholders, a few people. I see this to be an immoral contract sanctioned by the state. This is also fully supported by the current interpretation of the laws by lawyers and the courts as we had just discovered when some of us tried to buy Ben & Jerry's. I asked him what he thought we should do about this situation.

He replied, "Terry, I am here for another five years or so and then I am gone. My job during that time is to increase the value to the shareholders. What you are talking about is not my business."

By this time I had become so comfortable in my relationship with him that I respectfully responded, "Then no human being is leading Unilever? You too are working for the immoral contract?"

A bit startled, he looked at me and simply replied again, "That is not something with which I have anything to do. My job is to increase the value to the shareholders."

I went into a state of shock.

Thankfully at this point, Pierre Ferrari, one of my fellow board members interjected with something like, "Do you support a particular professional soccer team in England?"

This was a profound experience for me. I had just spent three hours with this man and discovered he was a very bright and caring person. He loved his wife and children and was very involved in his local community, active in the equivalent of coaching Little League Baseball.

Yet it was also obvious that there was no way he or any person could graduate up the ranks of a multinational corporation if not totally dedicated, with religious passion, to giving priority to maximizing the financial interests of the shareholders. That meant that it was at the expense of the customers, workers, communities, suppliers and the environment. That is, it was at the expense of the common good.

As I sat there drinking my decaf coffee I realized that this was the case in every multinational corporation on Earth and I became very concerned for Earth and all of its children, animals, and plants. It was instantly clear to me that if we did not soon mature into common good capitalism, especially by these multinational organizations with all of their power and muscle, we could be in great danger.

I recently read that fifty-one of the one hundred largest economies on the planet are multinational corporations. Only forty-nine are nations. What is significant is that the percentage of the one hundred largest economies being multinationals is increasing. I have also read that around half of all outstanding shares of U.S. corporations are now also held by corporations operating on the same philosophy: pension funds, mutual funds, insurance companies, banks, foundations, and university endowments. Also, as of this writing the largest five hundred companies in the USA are sitting on over $3 trillion in cash, and they believe they cannot legally spend it unless the priority is increasing their profits. That is, *according to their current way of thinking,* it cannot be spent where the priority is the common good. As I hope you now agree, this is an inaccurate and immature perception.

Suddenly it became clear to me that this immoral contract is increasingly and skillfully dominating the planet with no human beings inside those companies easily able to change this priority.

The next day, on the three hour drive home from Burlington, VT, the home of Ben & Jerry's, I took my third vow with myself: I would dedicate the rest of my life to understanding what we need to understand to be able to voluntarily mature out of this situation and into a more mature economic social order. I knew it had to be voluntary because we are now all beyond the Teen Layer of maturity. I also knew, therefore, that it had to be the result of a fundamental maturation of our skill of self-consciousness for it to be both voluntary and irresistible. Finally, I also was not aware of anyone who was coming at the challenge from this direction and I knew that this was the direction from which we needed to come to solve the problem. I also knew I was a deep student of spirituality, psychology, philosophy, economics, finance and business, and that no one had figured it out. Therefore, I had to ignore those worlds, stay in my house in the forest, and study my direct experience to find the answers. That was in July of 2000. This book is the result of my work since then to solve this problem in this way.

Each year the board of Ben & Jerry's goes to either London or Amsterdam for one of our board meetings and I have a chance to go to dinner with executives within Unilever. They are also always bright and caring people. Always late at night when all have become very relaxed, I ask them the same question I asked the Chairman-CEO. Like him, they nearly always agree with my analysis that the priority of the company is an immoral one. When I fish to see why they continue working for the company if they agree this am the case, their answers nearly always come down to some form of "I have to put my kids through college."

What is of particular concern is that on the one hand the multinational corporations are using the paternalism of the system to declare that they are not responsible for giving priority to the common good —"that is the government's job." By contract with it, metaphorically the parent, they are only responsible for giving priority to the financial interests of the shareholders because that is how they understand their contract with it.

At the same time they use all of their large amount of power, capital, and influence to move the governments to pass laws that support them giving priority to a few, to supporting what some believe in conversations is their immoral contract with the state. They justify not being responsible for the outcome because they are just doing their jobs within this *assumed* priority of their contract with the state and their responsibilities as members of a free society. Operating at the Adult Layer or lower they believe it is right and natural for them to primarily advocate for their self-interests.

I include the word "assumed" above because, as you now know, they *could* legally give priority to the common good. It is their Adult Layer of maturity, the giving of priority to an outside belief within the assumption that the universe is an immense number of separate parts, which has them assume it is wise and responsible to have their highest priority be the financial interests of a few, their shareholders. Actually themselves since a large portion of their compensation is in stock options.

The assumption is that we are each a separate part and competition is the fundamental process in nature, and therefore we naturally give priority to the self-interest of our physical bodies. A corporation is a contract with some people, mainly the shareholders, to give priority to their collective financial self-interests. Responsible behavior, they believe, is giving priority to honoring that contract.

My experience, especially now that I am part of a multinational, is that the people in multinationals are as well intentioned as other people.

It is the fundamental outside belief that is the problem.

We must build on true freedom. Therefore, we must provide the members of the boards and the executives of corporations a way to change to giving priority to the common good that makes sense to them. It also must not be polarized in their thinking with their personal self-interest or the self-interest of their companies.

Instead it must be obvious that it will significantly enhance both.

This can only occur when those in power each take back their own power, all of it, and, having thrown out all of their current beliefs, they study their immediate direct experience and realize that, indeed, it is self-evident that the universe is an indivisible whole.

They will then eventually conclude, "I will die but the universe will not die. Therefore by nature my highest priority is not just my personal maturation but also the maturation of us all, of the universe. This means to be personally happy I need to give priority to the common good in all I do, including in the running of our company."

Their personal maturation into the Elder and Mature Elder Layers, into true full freedom, is the only way this will happen.

The only other thing that could cause them to make changes in the way the company operates to accommodate this is responding to pressure from the wider society. But then, at least initially, it will only be for that purpose and not a genuine choice from having matured into the higher layers of maturity in the skill of self-consciousness. However, this maturation inside each of us is inevitable: maturation is the particular kind of cooperation that is the fundamental process in nature.

Changing the legal contract with the state is not necessary. Creating corporate law that explicitly states that the highest priority of the company is the common good would also be a step in the right direction, but it is not necessary. This has begun to happen in some states in the USA with the passage of "benefit corporate statutes" that allow social concerns to be on the same level of importance as financial concerns, even to take priority.

Corporate leaders can just affirm that their company is part of a global human society, as well as their state and national societies, and as a result they know that their highest priority is the common good or they have left them and are in competition with them.

They also know that this is not only best for all of life and humanity but also for the financial interests of their shareholders. Their financial highest priority is to survive. This will enable them to survive as humanity matures into the Elder Layer of maturity. It will also allow two companies' near duopoly monopoly relationship to survive. However it will only be able to be protected if the leaders of those companies are *genuinely* giving priority to the common good.

In addition everyone else also wins. The employees will be happier and more highly motivated. Now the genuine highest priority of the company is their highest priority as well, to be direct participants in the maturation of the universe. All will now be in total alignment. It will be the same with all of their suppliers, vendors, and partners.

Secondly, duopoly monopoly companies will be able to reach agreements with all their competitors to make the world a better place and be celebrated for doing so. And, *relative to one another,* it will not cost them a penny; if necessary they will both equally raise their costs to accommodate this. Any smaller competitor who tries to take advantage of this situation will be immediately called out by the press and on the Internet and they will have to join with the "product association guild" or receive the anger of the consumers. As a result they will quickly fall into alignment with their agreements.

By inviting common good audits by creditable third parties, all the activities of the organization can become transparent so the public will be able to witness if the executives have slid into giving priority to their self-interest by, for instance, providing inappropriate large salaries for themselves. The new openness by enterprises, both for-profit and non-profit and public and private, will allow for a public discussion of the appropriate level of compensation and forms of compensation for executives as well as the appropriate return to shareholders. More important, as happened with Mondragon, a very large conglomerate of worker-owned cooperatives in the Basque region of northern Spain that gives priority to the common good, executives will actively volunteer to take less personal income to be part of such an organization.

Companies can now work with all relevant parties to put a permanent end to poverty and irresponsible relationships with the environment. Also, local communities will very much want them to establish production facilities there.

Probably more important than all of the above, we will all experience the joy of the fundamental feeling of happiness when working in our companies. It will be our childhood work dream coming true. It will be like it was when I was working in Mollner's Meat Market.

As mentioned earlier, in 1979 I had the good fortune to spend a few months traveling throughout India living with and interviewing people still alive who had worked closely with Mahatma Gandhi. A delightful old man, elderly in every way, told me this story that he may have fabricated to make a point because I have never found evidence that it happened nor, frankly, have I searched for it. Either way, it is an edifying story that was his purpose in telling it to me.

He said Gandhi had an exchange in the 1940s with Mao Zetong, the founder of Communist China. Gandhi wrote Mao and told him he did not think his system would work. Mao wrote back and said, "But I am giving priority to the good of all the people." Gandhi wrote back and said, "Yes, it is very good that you are giving priority to the good of all the people. But you are having one group decide what is best for the good of all the people. The next stage in the development of humanity will build on individual freedom, not take it away."

We are ready to move beyond partial freedom, the giving of priority to an outside belief such as capitalism or communism, in the belief that it is an expression of full freedom. We are ready to mature into true full freedom.

That is where we keep our power, all of it, and primarily study our direct experience in the here and now and determine for ourselves the answer to these questions, "Is cooperation or competition the fundamental process in nature?" Then, "if we conclude that cooperation is the fundamental process in nature and it is when the parts give priority to the whole, is the universe an immense number of separate parts like our languages or is it an indivisible whole?" And "Is maturation the particular kind of cooperation that is the fundamental process in nature?"

If we conclude it is an indivisible whole, our true and mature self-interest is the self-interest of it. If we conclude that maturation is the particular kind of cooperation that is the fundamental process in nature, we have a new self-definition: "Each moment I am primarily the watcher and nurturer of the maturation of the universe." Or, to say it another way, "I give priority to participating in the love layer of maturity of cooperation and maturation."

We have now identified the accurate most fundamental truth and have also kept all of our power. Thus, each moment in the future we will be able to exercise our ability and right of individual free choice because we do not have to accommodate a second party, an outside belief. We are now each primarily a personal scientist who has achieved full freedom.

However it is important to note that our *personal maturation* into the mastery of the full skill of self-consciousness is just the beginning of our maturation, not the end. It is just a step in the progression toward the discovery that our true self-interest is the continuous maturation of the universe. Thus, between achieving full maturity in the skill of self-consciousness and death we have a new priority: eldering. And there is nothing more enjoyable than each moment giving priority to whatever is the best unique action we can take for the maturation of us all, the universe. Now we will spend the rest of our lives becoming self-consciously engaged in the maturation of our consensus agreements on Earth so our children will be born into a more mature consensus.

Once we know a more mature way of being in the world, whether it is riding a bicycle, using chopsticks, or using the human skill of self-consciousness, we can't resist consistently doing it the more mature way and turning it into a habit. Maturation is the fundamental process in nature.

As a species we are now ready for widespread maturation into the Elder and Mature Elder Layers of the skill of self-consciousness. One way or the other, using the words in this book or other words, we will each mature into freely choosing wherever we are standing to give priority to watching and nurturing the maturation of the universe.

As our priority as individuals matures, so will the priority of our organizations mature. One of the results will be the maturation of capitalism business into common good business.

In summary, lets imagine that you, the reader, other readers, and I are elders of our now global village. We also understand and agree with what has been written in this book. I think we would want to be active participants in what we can label for now a "Common Good Capitalism Movement," or more broadly perhaps the "Common Good Movement."

It would probably have three primary missions:

1. **End extreme poverty on Earth** using a private sector program (no budget cuts possible) by harnessing our financial markets,
2. **Locally re-village our lives** to more easily elder our children to full maturity in the skill of self-consciousness before they leave home, and

3. **Establish common good business** as an attractive option in the private sector.

As elders our first priority is to have all in our village have enough food, clothing, and shelter. Trusts for All Children could eventually accomplish this. Our second priority is to make sure our children are eldered to full maturity in the skill of self-consciousness before they leave home and especially before they marry.

Without the need for eldering there is not a need for elders. Without the need for elders there is not a need for community. We now know of the need for eldering and elders and therefore we will seek to re-village our lives in a modern context so we can make sure we directly and fully accomplish this most important task of parenting and eldering. After the ending of poverty there is nothing that is best simultaneously for our children and the common good.

Lastly, we want to encourage all of our for-profit and non-profit organizations to freely choose to give priority to the common good as a result of their leaders and members having achieved full maturity in the skill of self-consciousness. In whatever way we can participate in making this happen we want to play a role.

Additional missions may be that in our governments we play a role in the maturation of democracy into common good democracy. This is where over time we as citizens build toward consensus positions on concerns. Some may even want to form nations by agreement as a way for like-minded people to band together to accomplish in the private sector what is not ready to be embraced by the public sector.

I invite everyone who is reading this to become a participant in this movement by taking whatever you judge to be your best unique actions however large or small. If you would like involvement with others locally or beyond, or perhaps initially just monitor how this movement is growing, I invite you to go to our website: www.commongoodcapitalism.org.

Afterword

THE FIRST WORD WAS CREATED BY TWO HUMAN BEINGS looking each other in the eyes while each had a hand on a coconut or something else and saying to each other many times "wacko wacko" or something else. Without a language the only way they could have *agreed* to use the word "wacko" to represent a coconut was to have experienced oneness together (the absence of the possibility of conflict). Today when this happens locally—between two or more people—we call it "an agreement" (the local experience of oneness, the absence of the possibility of conflict).

However when the first word was created the agreement was experienced as everywhere. There was not yet an awareness in thinking of separate parts (time and space) that was the fundamental unconscious assumption necessary to create a word for the coconut.

The agreement was occurring within the reality of oneness that allowed it to occur. As is still the practice today, the mutual experience of peace instead of conflict is recognized as the experience of agreement.

Today many are still living as if one of the middle layers of maturity in the skill of self-consciousness is the highest layer. These are the layers where it is still assumed that the universe, like the words in a human language, is an immense number of separate parts and we are each one of them. They have not discovered and mastered the last two layers where they use the skills of a human language and the self-consciousness it allows to self-consciously enjoy the universe as an indivisible whole.

When these last two layers are discovered the *experience* is usually labeled "love." Not something between two people (relative love) but something that is everywhere at all times, like the wavelength of a radio channel, and is simultaneously and self-consciously being given priority by two or more people at the same time. Doing this is living at the highest possible layer of maturity of the skill of self-consciousness.

This experience is the experience of true love.

As a human species we are now ready to personally and organizationally graduate into living at the highest two layers of maturity of this skill.

At the personal level many of us have reached the extremes of giving priority to individual freedom (Teen Layer) by, for instance, choosing our romantic lover without the assistance of elders. If they were present and we respected them as elders, they would assist us to be sure we both had reached the highest layer of maturity in the skill of self-consciousness before we married. This is where we would both know the skill of true love. However part of going to extremes of giving priority in our societies to our ability and right of individual freedom is that such elders do not usually exist or if they do they are not respected as such.

This is a good thing!

In the absence of relationships with mature elders we only search for the next layer of maturity when we have gone to extremes of relying on the current one and it still has not ended thinking pain.

Many of us have also graduated to the next layer where we think things through and give priority to a fundamental outside belief (Adult Layer). We have gone to extremes of living according to our freely chosen fundamental outside belief and discovered it also is not bringing us the consistent experience of happiness we intuitively know is possible.

This is also a good thing! Thinking pain is always a gift. It demands that we search for and find each next layer until we have found the highest layer.

As the human species we are now ready to search for and find the next layer of maturity in the skill of self-consciousness. This is where we discover we have been giving our power to a second thing (a belief, a bunch of mutually agreed upon illusions within a human language). Now we know there is not a second thing to receive our power (Elder Layer).

This has us eventually discover the difference between partial and full freedom and to choose full freedom (Mature Elder Layer).

We discover and master these last two layers as skills by keeping our power and using it to study our direct experience to identify our most fundamental belief (personal science). There it is self-evident that cooperation is the fundamental process in nature and maturation is the particular kind of cooperation that is the fundamental process in nature. Therefore, *the universe is a maturing indivisible whole.* We are each first it that will not die and secondly our physical bodies that will die.

Also from the inside we each have sole and complete control of our physical bodies. Thus it is natural for us at all times, in all we do, and from where we are each standing to give priority to the maturation of the universe. We are going somewhere, not primarily in the mutually agreed upon illusion tool of separate parts (time and space) but in maturation. Where it will take us in terms of time and space we do not exactly know other than it will ultimately be maturation from where we are now, at a minimum a consistent maturation of our human consensus agreements on Earth.

Since we know that human languages (separate parts) are mutually created illusion tools, we now give priority each moment to the *experience of the oneness of nature, the experience of the universe being our physical body.* We then take whatever action is the best unique action we can take for the maturation of the universe. This has been called "eldering" and when giving it priority in our actions we experience the consistent happiness we have known all along to be our birthright. Life is now *experienced* as *meaningful and enjoyable.*

While fully doing both, with our competitors in business we give priority to *freely chosen common good agreements* and second priority to *competition.* So the public can be in a continuous conversation with our companies on what is giving priority to the common good for our times we will provide the public annual common good audits prepared by creditable third parties.

This will be the beginning of organizing our economy on Earth based on an awareness and embrace of the higher layers of maturity of the skill of self-consciousness.

As described earlier, if we are walking along a river, we see a small child drowning, we know how to swim, and there are no others around, without hesitation we jump into the river and bring the child to safety. It is so obvious this action is for the common good that we can't resist doing it. It is the natural and effortless action of knowing we are all in this together as parts of an indivisible whole.

Those who have achieved at least the Elder Layer of maturity know how to jump into the river and bring our economy to the safety of common good business. It is so obvious that this action is for the common good that they will not be able to resist doing it. Today there are many, and more each day, operating at the Elder Layer of maturity of the skill of self-consciousness. Therefore common good business is inevitable.

Giving Priority to What We Know

Without wisdom
Everything we see is not real.
Our human languages
Are between us and what we see.
Therefore, we see separate
As well as different parts.

The universe is an indivisible whole
But we cannot see oneness.
We can only know it is real.

The Rose on the Cover

The rose on the cover is what my father, Hienie Mollner, would draw next to his name each time he signed a note or card with a gift.

When anyone asked him what it meant he would say, "That rose is always watching to be sure you are following your conscience."

The three leaves represented the Father, Son, and Holy Spirit in his Catholic tradition. For me they represent the three dimensions of the skill of self-consciousness: recognition of differences, the mutual illusion tool of a human language that allows us to become self-conscious, and the oneness of nature. For all we know, since nothing was written down for over 60 years, these may have been the original generic meaning of the Son (recognition of differences), the Holy Spirit (the mutual illusion tool of human language that allows us to self-consciously participate in the maturation of the universe), and the Father (the oneness of nature): the three dimensions of the skill of self-consciousness.

About the Author

Terry Mollner, in the 1970s, was one of the earliest pioneers of socially responsible and community investing. A founder of the Institute for Community Economics (ICE), he guided fifteen leaders from around the country in the writing of one of the first set of social screens for investing. With Wayne Silby, one of those leaders, they used those screens to establish the Calvert Family of Socially Responsible Mutual Funds (www.calvert.com), the first family to such funds. Today the Calvert Group is one of the largest with $12 billion under management.

The team at ICE was also the creators of one of the first "community development financial institutes (CDFIs)" that make loans to low income housing projects, social and cooperative enterprises in low income communities, and microloan programs (small uncollateralized business loans). Today similar funds exist in communities throughout the US and are supported by annual funding from the US Government. This led Dr. Mollner to take the lead to create the Calvert Foundation (www.calvertfoundation.org) to raise capital from investors to fund this industry. It has raised and loaned over $1 billion to reduce poverty around the world and is one of the largest contributors of capital to the growth to this movement. Dr. Mollner continues to serve on the board of both Calvert organizations.

In 2000 he stepped up to assist Ben & Jerry's (www.benjerry.com) in its need to be bought by a multinational to deal with its distribution need as it was becoming a global brand. As part of its purchase by Unilever, he and the board arranged for a contract that allowed Ben & Jerry's to both continue to operate as an independent company and have a contract that obligated Unilever to allow it to continue to spend the same percentage of its annual budget on social activism as of the year it was bought. Ben & Jerry's is the only socially responsible company from the last half of the 20th century bought by a multinational to sign such a contract. Terry has been on its board since its purchase in 2000. Recently, Unilever also used this model in its purchase of Seventh Generation.

Dr. Mollner is also a founder and chair of Stakeholders Capital (www.stakeholderscapital.com), a socially responsible asset management firm with offices in Massachusetts, Illinois and California. Since 1973 he has been the founder and executive director of Trusteeship Institute (www.commongoodmovement.com). Its current project is the creation of Trusts for All Children (www.trustsforallchildren.org), a membership program to create a trust for poor children around the world as well as trusts for the children of members. He is also the author of *The Love Skill: We Are Each Mastering the 7 Layers of Human Maturity* and two books and many articles on the Mondragon Cooperatives in the Basque Region of northern Spain.

As part of his experiments to learn more about re-villaging our lives in a modern context, he is one of the founders of three intentional re-villagings that continue to exist: Spanish House, Hearthstone Village, and Friends and Lovers Community.